SNOWDONIA: SOUTH
30 LOW-LEVEL AND
EASY WALKS

FROM FFESTINIOG TO THE DYFI, AND BALA TO THE COAST

by Alex Kendall

JUNIPER HOUSE, MURLEY MOSS,
OXENHOLME ROAD, KENDAL, CUMBRIA LA9 7RL
www.cicerone.co.uk

© Alex Kendall 2020
First edition 2020
ISBN: 978 1 85284 985 6

Printed in China on responsibly sourced paper on behalf of Latitude Press Ltd
A catalogue record for this book is available from the British Library.
All photographs are by the author unless otherwise stated.

© Crown copyright 2020 OS PU100012932

Updates to this Guide

While every effort is made by our authors to ensure the accuracy of guide-books as they go to print, changes can occur during the lifetime of an edition. Any updates that we know of for this guide will be on the Cicerone website (www.cicerone.co.uk/985/updates), so please check before planning your trip. We also advise that you check information about such things as transport, accommodation and shops locally. Even rights of way can be altered over time. We are always grateful for information about any discrepancies between a guidebook and the facts on the ground, sent by email to updates@cicerone.co.uk or by post to Cicerone, Juniper House, Murley Moss, Oxenholme Road, Kendal, LA9 7RL.

Register your book: To sign up to receive free updates, special offers and GPX files where available, register your book at www.cicerone.co.uk.

Front cover: Looking out over the Mawddach estuary from the New Precipice Walk on an autumn evening (Walk 11)

CONTENTS

Debris in the woodland of the Cynfal gorge, a special place for mosses and ferns (Walk 1)

Route symbols on OS map extracts

(for OS legend see printed OS maps)

N

	route	(SF)	start/finish point
	alternative/link route	(S)	start point
◀	direction of walk	(F)	finish point

0 ½ mile

0 1km

Route maps at 1:50,000 scale unless otherwise stated

Walk no	Walk	Start
Around the Rhinogydd		
1	Ceunant Cynfal	Llan Ffestiniog
2	Rhaeadr y Cwm	near Llan Ffestiniog
3	Tomen y Mur	near Trawsfynydd
4	Llyn Trawsfynydd	Trawsfynydd
5	Harlech	Harlech
6	Llanbedr	Llanbedr
7	Black Falls	Ganllwyd
8	Pistyll Cain	near Ganllwyd
The Mawddach Estuary		
9	Barmouth	Barmouth
10	Mawddach to Ysgethin	Bontddu
11	New Precipice Walk	Llanelltyd
12	Precipice Walk	near Dolgellau
13	Foel Offrwm	near Dolgellau
14	The Mawddach Estuary	Penmaenpool
15	Morfa Mawddach and the Blue Lake	near Fairbourne
Bala to Dolgellau		
16	Brithdir	near Brithdir
17	Foel Caerynwch	Brithdir
18	Afon Melau	Rhydymain
19	Llyn Arenig Fawr	near Llyn Celyn
20	Afon Lliw	near Llanuwchllyn
21	Gwastadros	near Bala
22	Bala Lake/Llyn Tegid	Llangower
Cadair Idris to the Dyfi		
23	Cwm Cywarch	Dinas Mawddwy
24	Castell y Bere	near Abergynolwyn
25	Abergynolwyn	Abergynolwyn
26	Birds' Rock	Dolgoch
27	Dolgoch Falls	Dolgoch
28	Cwm Ratgoed	Corris
29	Aberdyfi	Aberdyfi
30	Machynlleth	Machynlleth

Distance	Ascent	Walking time	Page
			23
5.5km (3½ miles)	350m	1hr 45min	24
7km (4¼ miles)	220m	2hr 15min	29
9km (5½ miles)	240m	2hr 45min	34
12.5km (7¾ miles)	100m	3hr 15min	39
8.8km (5½ miles)	200m	2hr 30min	43
8km (5 miles)	200m	2hr 30min	48
6km (3¾ miles)	220m	2hr	54
3km (1¾ miles)	50m	1hr	59
			63
9km (5½ miles)	340m	3hr	64
12.5km (7¾ miles)	500m	4hr	69
12km (7½ miles)	450m	3hr 45min	74
5.5km (3¼ miles)	50m	1hr 30min	80
4 km (2½ miles)	100m	1hr 15min	83
18.5km (11½ miles)	350m	5hr 15min	86
13km (8 miles)	360m	4hr	92
			97
12km (7½ miles)	450m	4hr	98
3.4km (2¼ miles)	170m	1hr 15min	103
11km (6¾ miles)	340m	3hr 15min	107
10km (6 miles)	130m	2hr 45min	112
12km (7½ miles)	340m	3hr 45min	117
6km (3¾ miles)	200m	2hr	122
7.5km (4¾ miles)	250m	2hr 30min	125
			131
11km (6½ miles)	160m	3hr	132
7km (4½ miles)	120m	2hr	137
8.3km (5¼ miles)	290m	2hr 45min	141
10.5km (6¾ miles)	270m	3hr 15min	145
2.6km (1¾ miles)	120m	1hr	149
13.3km (8¼ miles)	200m	4hr	152
13km (8 miles)	300m	4hr	157
14.5km (9 miles)	300m	4hr 15min	161

The ruined wall of 13th-century Castell Carndochan with Llyn Tegid on the horizon (Walk 20)

A range of sand dunes covered in marram grass stands between Harlech and the sea (Walk 5)

INTRODUCTION

Snowdonia National Park encompasses the highest mountains in Wales, hugely popular for walking and climbing. But the area is far more than just the high peaks. Far below the soaring summits are beautiful woodlands, tranquil valleys and rambling paths to thundering waterfalls. And perhaps the most surprising thing for people who have only ventured here to climb Snowdon, is that these hills are a coastal mountain range, with miles of sand dunes, unspoilt beaches and cliffs.

The southern part of the national park is a wild place, less visited than the north, but bigger, with vast moorlands and mountain crags interspersed with incredible views, where lowland walkers can discover the beauty of the area just as much as people who head to the summits. The nature of low-level walking is that it can be done at any time of year, in pretty much all weathers, and normally within easy reach of a way out. On a grim day after rain the sight of a thundering waterfall is much easier to appreciate than a hilltop covered in fog.

You'll also find history and culture in the landscape, from cairns dating back thousands of years to the Bronze Age, to Iron Age forts and the remains of the Roman occupation. From the middle ages, Welsh castles defend the valleys, while English castles hug the coast, and old estates are still haunted by memories of rebellions. Into the modern era, we see mines on the hillsides, now slowly being taken over by vegetation, and the success of the modern tourist industry in bringing people and investment to the area (which means of course pubs and cafés!). But this is a landscape still moulded by sheep farming and forestry, where traditions continue that have been going on for hundreds of years.

The region encompassed in this book formed the old county of Meirionydd, dissolved in 1996 and now part of Gwynedd. The area within this guidebook has a northern boundary at the Vale of Ffestiniog. Moving south it includes the vast upland of the Migneint and the mountains of the Arenig range in the north-east, across Bala Lake and over the Aran range in the south-east. In the west it follows the coast around the Rhinogydd and includes the Mawddach and Dyfi Estuaries, separated by Cadair Idris and the Tarrens. The southern boundary is the edge of the national park, including Machynlleth. It is a big place, and the walking opportunities are endless. These 30 walks give a brilliant flavour of the area, head to all the famous points as well as some infrequently visited haunts. It will immerse you in the wildest and roughest landscape in Wales.

and lowlands, rather than heading up mountains. However, there are some stretches of the walks that run over hillsides and moorland, and there are even a few minor hilltops reached. The gradients and exposure on these walks is still far less than you'd experience up a mountain. What these walks are not, however, is flat. They are steady and mostly straightforward to navigate, but we are in mountainous country after all!

The aim in deciding which 30 walks to include comes from trying to spread them as equally as possible over southern Snowdonia, while including famous spots that I didn't want people to miss. A few are creations from scratch, where a general area seemed too beautiful to miss out, but where an established walk isn't obvious. These are often the ones that include one or two fiddly directions!

The result is a series of walks that will take people interested in exploring the valleys and coast of Snowdonia on 30 adventures with something new on each one. Whether you are looking for an hour or a day out, and whether you're a keen lowland walker, a mountaineer on a bad weather day, or a family out for a stroll, there are many places in here for you to explore.

THE WALKS

The terms 'low-level' and 'easy' can mean different things to different people. In general what these walks always aim to do is explore the valleys

LANDSCAPE

What you see when you look out over the mountains of Snowdonia is a landscape that has been affected by thousands of years of human activity, and millions of years of geological turmoil.

The oldest rocks in Snowdonia are the Rhinogydd, a key range of the southern part of the national park and an inspiring set of dark craggy towers. The sandstone, siltstone and mudstone that make up these peaks was deposited under the sea in the Cambrian period, from 528–508 million years ago. The following period, the Ordovician, which began around 485 million years ago, saw volcanic activity that created all the mountains that surround the Rhinogydd. Beginning with Rhobell Fawr, the first volcano in this cycle, all of the distinctive mountains that form the heartland of the area are Ordovician in origin.

To understand what followed, it's important to appreciate that Cambrian rock still lies underneath all the Ordovician mountains we see today, and that Ordovician rock used to lie on top of the Cambrian Rhinogydd.

Next came the Silurian period, where yet more rock was laid down. It was during the period after this – the Devonian, 419–358 million years ago – that pressure was applied on an enormous scale to raise these beds of rock up to become mountains. Initially Himalayan in height, the centre of this giant region of uplift was known as the Harlech Dome. The higher peaks at the centre of the dome were weathered faster, their rock being washed into the sea as sediment, and as the younger rock from the Silurian was exposed at the top, this was eroded first, followed by the Ordovician rock underneath. We are currently living at a time where

There are scattered trees on the walk, but Fœl Offrwm is mostly open hillside, with fantastic views (Walk 13)

The head of Cwm Cywarch is dominated by crags of Glasgwm (Walk 23)

there is almost no Silurian rock at all left in Snowdonia, and the Ordovician rock has gone from the central part of what was the Harlech Dome, now the Rhinogydd.

The most well-known big scale events of this weathering and erosion are the Ice Ages. We have had quite a few Ice Ages in the past few million years, each leaving its mark and gouging further into the mountains. Glaciers spill down from the mountains and take rocks far from their sources. Cwms and arêtes are formed, and the depressions left by the heads of glaciers form upland lakes. The pressure released by the melting ice caused rock-falls from cliffs that still go on to this day, assisted by continuing freeze-thaw, and can be seen in the large piles of rubble beneath crags.

Alongside the eye-catching forms of the high peaks, geology has left Snowdonia with many side effects of the different rock types and Ice Ages. The plateau moorland of the Migneint is where the ice cap is thought to have rested, leading to the lack of prominent peaks. The alternation between hard and soft rock in bedding planes, combined with the uplift of the land has led to the beautiful waterfalls and streams that cut through the valleys. Fault lines like that running south-west from Bala have eroded faster, leading to great valleys and ribbon lakes. And the golden estuaries have been formed by this eroded rock being deposited as Wales' well-known rainfall transports the mountains bit by bit into the sea.

HISTORY

People have been living in Snowdonia for thousands of years; from when the standing stones were lifted and the burial cairns were built on the prominent peaks and passes, such as Bwlch y Rhiwgyr. The climate back then was warmer and drier, and the trees grew right up to some of the mountain summits. As the Bronze Age became the Iron Age, Celtic tribes such as the Ordovicians moved in from the east, creating the hill forts that form such familiar features of the summits of Foel Offrwm and Pared y Cefn hir.

The Iron Age tribes were a brief match for the Romans, who begun their invasion of Wales in 48CE and completed it in 78CE with the final conquest of the north and of Anglesey, the power base of the druids. The Romans created a series of forts and roads, which in this area can especially be seen at Tomen y Mur and Brithdir. Despite governing Britain for hundreds of years, the Romans left at the end of the 4th century to leave Britain in what has become known as the Dark Ages.

The next few hundred years saw the arrival of the Saxons, who pushed the Britons west into Wales and Cornwall, and the start of Viking raids. The Romans had introduced Christianity, which flourished, and was supplemented in Snowdonia by the arrival of missionaries from Ireland. Wales then was not a united kingdom, but rather a series of princedoms with individual power bases.

When the Normans invaded England in 1066, they did not find it easy to subjugate Wales. The fort at Tomen y Mur was thought to be a Norman response to Gruffydd ap Cynan's uprising in 1095, and

The Mawddach Estuary from the coast road near Barmouth (Walk 9)

Harlech Castle seen from the sand dunes (Walk 5)

Llywelyn ap Iorwerth's grip on Wales was so secure in 1200, from his power base in Gwynedd, that the English King John signed a treaty with him. Llywelyn the Great, as he became known, built many of the Welsh castles we can see in the interior, including at Castell y Bere.

Llywelyn's grandson, Llywelyn ap Gruffudd, continued hostilities with the English, and the rising power of the Marcher Lords in the borderlands, but Edward I had enough and invaded Wales in 1283. The castles that dot the coast, including Harlech, were his way of stopping the Welsh from rebelling again, but barely 100 years later they did so, crowning Owain Glyndŵr as Prince of Wales in 1404. His 15-year rebellion, which utilised the rough ground of Snowdonia to hide troops, included the capture of

Harlech Castle, defeats of English armies, and the signing of a treaty with France. Famously, he was never captured, and there is still doubt over his fate.

In 1485, following the Battle of Bosworth, Harri Tudur, a Welshman, became King of England as Henry VII. His son, Henry VIII, further united England and Wales with the Laws in Wales Acts, but though the two countries were closer than ever, the Welsh still retained their language and customs. For the next few hundred years, peace developed between the countries of Britain, and industry grew, particularly shipbuilding on the estuaries of Snowdonia and the continued mining of metals in the mountains.

In the 18th and 19th centuries, the slate boom took off in North

Wales, as giant mines opened with the finance and infrastructure to ship the finished product around the world. A gold rush also kicked off in the valleys around the Mawddach, and slowly as roads were built, tourism began, with botanists, geologists and diarists leading the way for walkers and climbers. As the Napoleonic Wars of the early 19th century closed off travel to much of mainland Europe, aristocrats began tours of the 'British Alps' where they would climb Snowdon and Cadair Idris, and marvel at the waterfalls.

After the World War 1, when Britain nearly ran out of timber, the Forestry Commission was created, taking over and afforesting vast areas beginning in the 1920s, and providing employment just as the slate industry was shrinking

due to overseas competition and cheap imports. Sheep farming on the mountains was and continues to be a major land use here, in areas well above suitable forest land, and in the valleys you'll spot the charismatic Welsh Black Cattle.

The drive for access to the mountains and moorlands of the UK led to the creation of national parks. Snowdonia was one of the first, created in 1951 to protect the landscape and to get people into the outdoors. The massive growth in all outdoor activities, from walking and climbing to mountain biking and kayaking, has seen Snowdonia become one of the most popular sites for these activities in the UK. Alongside the national park, conservation organisations are involved in many different ways to protect the landscapes of Snowdonia,

Disused mine buildings are dwarfed by the crags of Craig-y-cae (Walk 7)

from the Woodland Trust's ownership of several beautiful woodlands to large-scale schemes such as the Dyfi Biosphere Reserve.

WILDLIFE

The diversity of landscape types in south Snowdonia means the area is a great place to see all sorts of wildlife. Despite centuries of persecution by landowners and gamekeepers, you will have wildlife encounters if you look hard enough, and pick the right time of year.

On the mountains and moorlands, though the vegetation has been reduced to predominantly mat

A scarlet tiger moth in the hills near Machynlleth (Walk 30)

grass and soft rush by grazing pressure, there are moorland birds such as curlew, snipe and buzzards, and you may spot a badger or a fox. Individual trees cling on to crags and gullies, including rowan and hawthorn, and now and then the bright yellow flowers of gorse will brighten up a day even in the middle of winter.

Among the admittedly large tracts of non-native conifer plantation, there are plenty of broadleaved woodlands, many of which classify as Celtic rainforests. These oak-dominated woodlands are home to hundreds of species of mosses, ferns and liverworts, especially in the deep gorges, as well as a variety of small birds and fungi. The mushrooms that you see growing near trees are just the fruiting bodies (like flowers) of a

The spring bluebell display in Coed Isaf (Walk 16)

much larger organism underground. We are beginning to understand how fungi work in synchrony with trees, forming a giant network for protection and to gather resources. Being in one of these ancient woodlands, such as those on the side of Ceunant Cynfal or Coed Aber Artro, can take you back in time to when druids strode the land.

The estuaries and coast are important places for wading birds such as oystercatchers, feeding on the crustaceans and worms that live in the sand. There can often be wildflowers like orchids and stonecrops in the dunes and along rocky embankments, and the marshes and wetlands are popular spots for migratory geese. If you are very lucky you may see dolphins out in the bay!

The most distinctive site for seeing wildlife is Birds' Rock, especially in the spring. It is a place where all sorts of birds nest, including peregrine falcons, but it is probably most well-known for seeing the chough, a type of crow that is present in Snowdonia in greater numbers than elsewhere in the UK. It is also home to the largest inland colony of cormorants in Wales, and you'll easily notice these large black seabirds if they soar slowly overhead.

Summer brings the purple of heather to the hills and the yellow of bog asphodel and tormentil to moorland. Autumn brings the golden leaves of the birch in the setting sun, and winter brings the grey and black flocks of geese to the water, and snow to the mountain summits. It is important to remember that even common species can add a lot to a day out. Listen out for the song of the skylark in spring or a glimpse of a thrush darting through woodland.

If you want to help protect the wildlife in the area, please do not disturb any animals, and do not pick wildflowers. To help further, please consider donating to the North Wales Wildlife Trust (www.northwales wildlifetrust.org.uk).

be occasions where snow or ice may affect the walks in winter, and ice can form even at a low level. Likewise, flooding does occur in some areas and may lead to you needing to change your plans. But throughout the year Snowdonia remains open and inviting for walkers and each season has its own charms.

WHEN TO GO

Most of the walks in this book, being low-level, can be done at any time of year. They are all excellent in the warmth of summer, but they are still accessible in the depth of winter or in foul weather when the mountain summits are beyond the comfort zone of most people.

On a few of the walks that go onto low hills or moorland there may

GETTING THERE

Road

The southern part of Snowdonia has several points of entry. There are A roads coming west from Shrewsbury and Chester, and up from the south of Wales. These connect at some point to the north–south roads of the M5 and M6 motorways.

From the approach to Bwlch Rhiwgyr, Cadair Idris rises on the horizon (Walk 10)

Train

The main railway line comes west from Shrewsbury to Machynlleth and then goes up the coast via Aberdyfi, Barmouth and Harlech, and it is also possible to travel into this part of the national park from the other railway terminus at Blaenau Ffestiniog, which is on the line from Llandudno. The railway line is marked as a black line on the overview map.

Bus

Once in the park, the bus network is reasonably good, serving most valleys, even remote villages, throughout the year.

For more information and timetables for buses and trains, see www.traveline.cymru. Trains can also be booked at www.thetrainline.com.

ACCOMMODATION

There are plenty of places to stay throughout this part of the national park, despite it being less touristy than the north. The main towns are Bala, Machynlleth, Aberdyfi, Dolgellau and Harlech, with the valleys in-between hosting plenty of other options and everything from campsites to hotels. For a good selection, see www.visitsnowdonia.info, as well as the YHA website (www.yha.org.uk) and Independent Hostels website (www.hostelsuk.net) for hostel style accommodation.

WHAT TO TAKE

Despite the walks being low-level, it's important to stay warm and comfortable. The weather can change quickly in mountainous terrain, so it's sensible to take a bag with some key items with you even if you're only going out on a short walk. Don't forget the following:

- a set of waterproofs
- warm clothes
- a hat, gloves and a buff/scarf
- walking clothes
- walking socks
- comfortable outdoor shoes
- a bottle of water, and some food
- a small first aid kit
- a charged mobile phone
- a map, plus a compass
- a head torch – especially useful when walking in winter when the days are shorter, if you are out longer than you expect, or you want to start in the dark!

THE COUNTRYSIDE CODE

Please make sure you follow the Countryside Code when out and about, and respect whoever's land you're walking through. Close gates if you open them, and do not let your dog worry livestock, keeping it on a lead whenever anywhere near sheep. In bird-nesting season, remember that moorland birds are ground nesting, so keep your dog on a short lead.

Most importantly, do not drop any litter, including food waste such as peel and cores. Litter can harm wildlife and is an eyesore for other walkers, as well as potentially polluting the area.

MAPS AND GPS

The map extracts in this guidebook are from 1:50,000 OS maps, with a handful from 1:25,000 OS maps. Although many of the walks follow clear or waymarked routes, you may find it useful to have a 1:25,000 map with you. The relevant 1:25,000 map is indicated in the information box at the start of each route description. Alongside these two map scales, Harvey publishes a 1:40,000 map of South Snowdonia, which covers the whole of the area explored in this book (apart from Walk 30).

GPX tracks

GPX tracks for the routes in this guidebook are available to download free at www.cicerone.co.uk/985/GPX. A GPS device is an excellent aid to navigation, but you should also carry a map and compass and know how to use them. GPX files are provided in good faith, but neither the author nor the publisher accept responsibility for their accuracy.

WHAT3WORDS

Each walk in this book contains a 'what3words' address. What3words is an organisation that has allocated every 3m x 3m square in the world a unique three-word address. These addresses won't change. They therefore make it much easier for you to find obscure places where a postcode is too broad, such as laybys, countryside car parks, and other fiddly walk starting locations. It works just like a sat-nav. The what3words addresses given for each walk are indicated by /// and displayed next to the start/finish in the walk information box.

Download the what3words app onto your smartphone, enter the three words at the start of the walk, and you can use Google maps or OS maps on your phone (via the Viewranger app) to get you to exactly the right spot!

UNDERSTANDING WELSH PLACENAMES

It will help you follow the guidebook directions if you understand what certain Welsh words mean, especially those appearing on the map.

USEFUL TOPOGRAPHICAL WORDS

afon	river
nant	stream
cwm	cirque/raised valley
dyffryn	valley
moel(bald)	hill
coed	woodland
traeth	beach
rhaeadr/pistyll	waterfall
llyn	lake
craig	crag

SAFETY

Accidents can happen even on easy walks so it's good to have a plan of what to do in an emergency. Make sure you have a first aid kit and mobile phone with you, and if you are walking alone tell your accommodation or a friend where you're going. Ensure you can stay warm and comfortable if you have to stay in the same place in bad weather. If you have an accident away from a road, you can contact Mountain Rescue by calling 999 and asking for the police; they will then pass your information on to Mountain Rescue. Please remember that Mountain Rescue teams are made up of volunteers; consider making a donation to the local team when you see a collection tin!

USING THIS GUIDE

Each walk starts with an information panel summarising key planning information about the route including distance, ascent, terrain, and projected walking time. There are also details on how to find the start point and parking place (including the postcode), and any refreshments available locally.

Within the text, the spellings of the placenames used are those which correlate with the accompanying map extract. Features that appear on the route maps are marked in bold on their first use to help you see where you are on the map as you read through. Placenames that do not appear in bold may be taken from a different scale of OS map or another source altogether, or have already been mentioned.

Moel Llyfnant and Arenig Fawr dominate the skyline above Coed Wenallt (Walk 20)

Following the path along the southern bank of the Cynfal gorge

There is no 'difficulty' rating given for each walk, as difficulty means different things to different people. Instead, you should consider distance, ascent, projected time and terrain, to see if that walk is for you and your party.

AROUND THE RHINOGYDD

Cefn Coch gold mine and the view over Coed y Brenin (Walk 7)

Walk 1
Ceunant Cynfal

The gorge of Ceunant Cynfal plunges down through Ffestiniog, almost hidden from the road, and is a key sanctuary for wildlife. The wooded hillsides hide the Afon Cynfal, and this walk extends the simple out-and-back advocated by most websites into a better and slightly longer exploration of the lower gorge. Following paths through the woods, with the river below, it leads to Pont Tal-y-bont and back up through the woods on the far side before crossing the river again and visiting the famous Rhaeadr Cynfal waterfall, a famous tourist spot for the Victorians.

Llan Ffestiniog sits above the Cynfal gorge, with the Moelwynion behind

Start/finish	Y Pengwern, Llan Ffestiniog /// elbowed.rifled.theory
Distance	5.5km (3½ miles)
Ascent	350m
Time	1hr 45m
Terrain	Mostly small paths, with some sections of track
Maps	OS Explorer Map OL18 Harlech, Porthmadog & Bala/Y Bala
Access	Llan Ffestiniog lies on the A470 between Trawsfynydd and Blaenau Ffestiniog. The pub Y Pengwern has on-street parking outside and can be found at LL41 4PB.
Facilities	Llan Ffestiniog has a pub and a corner shop. More shops and places to eat are available in Blaenau Ffestiniog.

From the outside of the Y Pengwern pub in **Llan Ffestiniog**, head to the main road, the **B4391**, and turn right to walk downhill on the road, with the church on the right. After 50m, when the road bends right, go ahead onto a footpath, next to the 14% road sign. There is a signpost to the falls.

Soon, cross a track and go through a gate, continuing ahead straight down the field. Half-way down there is a footpath post and waterfall sign on the left – ignore these and continue straight down and through another gate, over a track and through the gate opposite.

Head down the next field, heading to the bottom right-hand corner. Go through two black metal gates and follow the level path through the trees (not the one going downhill). Follow this path for over 500m through **Coed Ty-isaf**, where there are views of the gorge in **Ceunant Cynfal** on the left. The gorge is a haven

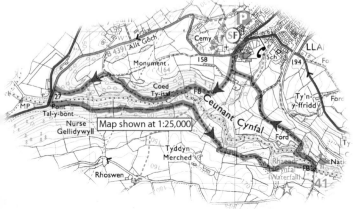

25

The trail takes you deep into the woodland of the Cynfal gorge

for hundreds of mosses, ferns and liverworts, many of which you will see as you make your way to the waterfall.

The path is level, then rises to leave the wood via a gate into a field. Cross the field, keeping the fence on the left. The field drops down the hill and a wall appears ahead; bear left when the fence does the same, keeping the wall on the right to head down to a stile. Cross it back into the woodland. The peak ahead is Moelwyn Bach, the most southerly hill of the Moelwynion range, which stretches all the way from here to Capel Curig.

Follow the path ahead, which soon joins a wider path downhill. After a few hundred metres, arrive at the road, the A496. Turn left onto the road to cross the bridge of **Pont Tal-y-bont** over the Afon Cynfal (be careful as there is no pavement). Turn left onto the path immediately after the bridge, where there are some fantastic chestnut trees in **Nurse Gellidywyll**.

This path continues on for around 1km until reaching a junction, where a footbridge is visible on the left. Continue straight on, staying on the right-hand side of the Afon Cynfal. The path leaves the woods but continues traversing. There are a few gates to pass, and you'll cross a small stream.

Eventually the path reaches a junction, with a footbridge over the Afon Cynfal on the left. Turn left and cross the bridge, continuing up the steps opposite and

The Afon Cynfal makes its way through the gorge

following the path ahead. After 50m there is a faint path on the left, starting beside a 'steep drop' sign. Take this path, which leads along the top of the gorge to the viewpoint of the **Rhaeadr Cynfal**.

Upstream from the waterfall stands **Huw Llwyd's pulpit**, a pillar of rock in the river. Huw lived around the 16th century and managed, according to local legend, to maintain the dual roles of clergyman and wizard, combining Christian teaching with an ability to cast spells. People would come and hear him as he sat on the pillar and preached, his voice able to miraculously carry above the sound of the thundering water. He would also cast out demons, who would be dashed against the rocks below the waterfall, giving it the alternative name of the Black Falls.

Beyond the waterfall, continue on the path up to the T-junction and turn left. Soon the path exits the woods via a gate beside an information board.

Go through the gate and follow the rising path up through several fields to a set of gates by a small barn. Go through the first gate, then follow the fence on the left to a small gate, where Llan Ffestiniog's church is visible ahead.

Go left, through the gate, and follow the path ahead to a small metal gate 100m away. Descend the path and cross the stream; beyond the gate, head onwards and up 50m to a footpath post in the field and continue on across the field to another metal gate. Once through this gate turn right, uphill, to return to Llan Ffestiniog.

Heading down through woodland from Llan Ffestiniog towards the Cynfal

Walk 2
Rhaeadr y Cwm

Exploring the moorland and gorge around the waterfall at Rhaeadr y Cwm, this walk visits Llyn Morwynion, mentioned in the Welsh myths of The Mabinogion, before dropping down to the Afon Cynfal. It follows the river upstream, and then after one steep climb gives a fantastic view up the ravine where the water plunges down from the Migneint. This is a reasonably straightforward walk with lots of interest and a far-reaching view down the Vale of Ffestiniog. Some paths can be obscure.

Crossing moorland above Cwm Cynfal, with the Moelwynion hills in the distance

Start/finish	Car park above gorge on the B4391 /// hedgehog.small.unstated
Distance	7km (4¼ miles)
Ascent	220m
Time	2hr 15min
Terrain	Countryside paths and tracks
Maps	OS Explorer Map OL18 Harlech, Porthmadog & Bala/Y Bala
Access	The car park is substantial but not well signposted. Head east from Llan Ffestiniog on the B4391 for roughly 2 miles. The car park is on the right as the gorge comes into view. Postcode is roughly LL41 4PT.
Facilities	None. Nearest shop and pub in Llan Ffestiniog.

From the **car park** next to the gorge on the **B4391**, head to the road and turn left. After 50m, turn right through the gate onto the footpath.

Follow the footpath ahead uphill, under the power line, and when it appears, across the ruined stone wall. Turn right on the track straight after the stone wall.

Follow the track up to **Llyn Morwynion** and continue until the fork by the 'no swimming' sign. Turn right to cross the **dam**.

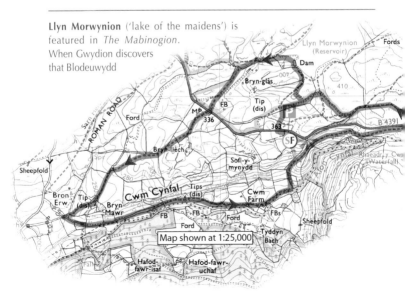

Llyn Morwynion ('lake of the maidens') is featured in *The Mabinogion*. When Gwydion discovers that Blodeuwydd

Llyn Morwynion, high on the Migneint

tried to get Gronw to kill her husband Lleu, he pursues her and her maidens from Mur Castle (at Tomen y Mur) over the Afon Cynfal and up to this lake. The maidens fall in and drown, but Gwydion spares Blodeuwydd, turning her instead into an owl as punishment so that she will never see daylight again. The peak across the lake is Y Garnedd – at 552m, it's one of the high points of the Migneint, the vast moor that spreads east and south from here.

Beyond the dam, follow the grassy path onwards. Step over the small stream and follow the lake edge. When the lake ends, continue ahead and go through the gate at the wall/fence corner. At the footpath post immediately after this, turn left, downhill.

Pass some crags and follow the stream down; look out for the old slate quarry on the left. Follow the path down the hillside and head to the gate in the stone wall when it appears below on the left. The ground here is quite rough.

Go through the gate and continue straight ahead on a faint path. The **B4391** road appears ahead, with metal footpath posts next to it; head straight for them. There is a stream to cross, with a small bridge. Cross the stile to the road, cross over, and continue ahead on the track nearly opposite.

When the track bends left towards a hut, leave the track and go straight ahead onto a faint path to the right of the mound and the stone wall. Follow this straight ahead. Soon, cross a ruined wall and carry on ahead next to a wall/fence. Follow

Rhaeadr y Cwm, dropping down from the Migneint into Cwm Cynfal

the fence down to a stile in the bottom corner with a yellow-topped post. Cross the stile. The view ahead opens out down the Vale of Ffestiniog to Tremadog Bay, with the Irish Sea shining in the distance (or obscured by rain).

Head through the next field, keeping the fence on the right until passing a mound, then bear left, when a footpath arrow points that way. Head towards the farm, and at the bottom of the field, head right past a stone ruin and an earth mound to find a track between two walls, with yellow arrows.

Go down the track, through the farm at **Bryn Mawr** to reach a T-junction with a tarmac track, Turn left and follow this track into **Cwm Cynfal**. Stay on the left side of the **Afon Cynfal** for about 1km to **Cwm Farm**, by which point the tarmac track has become stony. It is easy to see the difference between the small scraps of native woodland you're walking through, and the giant conifer plantation on Hafod fawr opposite.

On reaching the farm, go through the gate on the left with the footpath arrow, and continue past the farm buildings. Head through the field and rejoin the river, passing through a gate to continue doing so.

After the next stile/gate, cross to leave the field and turn left uphill on a vague grassy path. The going is steep, but continue up roughly following the fence. After 150m, and just before the small waterfall follow the path right. It soon levels off, leading to a **viewpoint** of the waterfall at **Rhaeadr y Cwm** and the gorge of the Afon Cynfal. In Welsh mythology it was on the banks of the Afon Cynfal that Gronw tried to kill Lleu, and where Lleu later came back to slay Gronw. The path leads gradually up towards the road, eventually running next to it.

Follow the fence to a metal kissing gate with a footpath post. Go through this and turn right on the road (so going in the same direction) and after 50m pass the **cattle grid** and turn left onto a footpath. The path then follows the fence.

After 150m cross the stile and continue following the fence on the left. The path soon bears away from the fence; follow it under the telegraph poles. The path is clear to follow, and almost leads back to Llyn Morwynion. On reaching a track junction, turn left, downhill.

Shortly, when the car park is visible on the left and there is a large mound on the right, turn left back onto the faint path from the start of the walk and follow it down the rough field back to the road. Turn left to reach the car park.

Walk 3
Tomen y Mur

Surely one of the most desolate postings in the Roman Empire, Tomen y Mur comprises a lot of history, from the Romans through the Dark Ages and the Norman Conquest right up to the Welsh princes and the mythology of The Mabinogion. Leading on to a larger circuit to give an impression of the fort's location in the landscape, this walk explores the remains of the fort before following trails through farmland and up onto the neighbouring hillsides, passing through a slate quarry and giving views over Llyn Trawsfynydd and the Rhinogydd. It is also possible to do a much shorter version of this walk that just explores the fort and grounds.

Tomen y Mur sits high on moorland in a lonely spot

Start/finish	Tomen y Mur car park /// expect.breathing.vast
Distance	9km (5½ miles) (or 1.5km (1 mile) if you just complete the short circuit of the Roman ruins)
Ascent	240m
Time	2hr 45min (or 30min)
Terrain	Farmland paths and upland tracks
Maps	OS Explorer Map OL18 Harlech, Porthmadog & Bala/Y Bala
Access	Despite being a key historical site, Tomen y Mur isn't signposted from the main road. To find it, head north out of Trawsfynydd on the A470. The turning is on the right, almost opposite the sign announcing the major right turn coming up towards Blaenau Ffestiniog. After turning right, the minor road goes under the old railway line. Keep following it up to the Tomen y Mur car park, which has a sign. The rough postcode is LL41 4RE.
Facilities	There is a café next to Llyn Trawsfynydd and a pub and corner shop in Trawsfynydd.

From the **car park** at Tomen y Mur – labelled '**Roman Amphitheatre**' on the 1:25,000 OS map – walk up the road (so the ruins are on the right). After 30m, turn right before the cattle grid, pass the information board and go through the small gate. The amphitheatre itself is on the left here. Follow the grassy path ahead, and after 100m, turn right at the footpath sign, heading towards the distinctive mound. The rough track here was the Roman road that led through the fort, connecting it to forts to the north and south and controlling movement through Wales.

Pass the *vicus*, the site of the Roman village, to reach a set of stone ruins, which mark the site of the old north-east gateway to the fort. Make your way through the ruins and up to the distinctive mound, which is the site of the Norman motte, built on top of the old **Roman fort**.

Turn right to go around it, which leads to extensive views over Llyn Trawsfynydd and the mountains of the Rhinogydd. Once you're most of the way round the mound, the path passes through a gap in a stone wall. Turn right after the gap and follow the ruined wall downhill. On reaching a bisecting wall, turn left, then soon right again to continue down to an information board on the site of the old bathhouse.

Facing the information board, turn right and follow the grassy path for 100m through a small gate to reach a sunken path. To complete the short circuit of

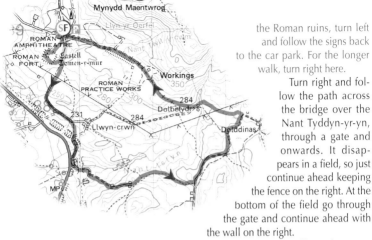

the Roman ruins, turn left and follow the signs back to the car park. For the longer walk, turn right here.

Turn right and follow the path across the bridge over the Nant Tyddyn-yr-yn, through a gate and onwards. It disappears in a field, so just continue ahead keeping the fence on the right. At the bottom of the field go through the gate and continue ahead with the wall on the right.

Join a track and continue ahead; the track soon bends left. Follow it for 400m, go through a gate and cross a stream in a wooded gully. Continue ahead, keeping the wall on the right and following a purple arrow. After 200m, carry on ahead through a gap in the wall and head up to the tarmac track. Turn right on this track to cross the bridge over the old railway.

Follow this track downhill, and just before reaching the main road, the **A470**, turn left through a gate onto a footpath, where there is a footpath sign on a post. Soon afterwards, pass through another gate and cross an old stone bridge over the **Nant Islyn**.

Continue up the tarmac track, passing under the railway arch and heading into the yard at Tyddyn Felin Farm. Once in the yard, turn left through a gate onto a stony track uphill through a field. Head through a gate at the top of the field to reach barns.

TOMEN Y MUR

A great example of Welsh literal naming, Tomen y Mur means 'mound in the walls', which is a very good description! The original Roman fort was built during the Roman conquest of Wales in 78CE to police the area against the Ordovices tribe and to link up other forts through Snowdonia. Abandoned in 140CE, the next notable structure is the mound, which is either a Dark Age Welsh structure or a Norman 'motte', the mound on which a wooden castle would have been built. The Normans certainly occupied the site from the

Crossing the bridge over the Nant Islyn

12th century onwards, perhaps in response to the Welsh uprising of 1095, led in part by the King of Gwynedd, Gruffydd ap Cynan.

The site was plausibly used by the future princes of Wales, including Gruffydd's grandson, Llywelyn the Great, but its most famous tale comes from Welsh mythology in *The Mabinogion*. As Mur Castle, it was the seat of Lleu, whose wife Blodeuwedd (who was created from flowers) plotted with her lover Gronw to have Lleu killed, which could only be carried out under extremely stringent circumstances. This accomplished, Gronw ruled over Lleu's lands, not knowing that Lleu had only been badly wounded. Brought back to full health, Lleu returned and challenged Gronw to stand at the same spot where he had tried to slay him. Gronw did so but hid behind a rock. Lleu threw his spear, which went straight through the rock and killed Gronw. Blodeuwedd meanwhile was turned into an owl as punishment for her sins, so she would never again show her face in daytime.

Go through the gate on the right-hand side of the barns and follow the track behind them, which immediately bends left; continue ahead with the fence on the left.

After 200m, on reaching a ruin, head to the gate on the right with the yellow arrow post; head through the gate and turn left to continue along the wall. The

Llyn Trawsfynydd, with the nuclear power station currently being dismantled

view left from this section shows the commanding position Tomen y Mur has in the landscape. The motte is clear on the hilltop.

After 500m the wall becomes a fence, and after 50m of the fence follow the path as it bends right, away from it, heading vaguely towards a farm at Bwlch-gwyn-uchaf.

The path heads around a rise, bending left up to a gate. Go through it and ahead through two more gates to reach a track (the farm is now over on the right). Turn left and follow this track up onto the moorland. At a track fork after roughly 1km, turn left and follow the track under the power lines.

The track becomes mud and grass; follow it to cross the Nant Islyn via a ford near **Dolbelydr**. Soon after the stream at a path fork, go right, uphill. It is quite eroded, but follow it closely across moorland. Becoming a track, it goes straight through the **slate quarry workings** at Braich-ddû (marked as disused on the map but now operational again). The track past this point follows the line of the old quarry railway, built in the 19th century. Once through the quarry the track continues on past **Llyn yr Oerfel** to reach the road. Turn left on the road and you'll soon reach the car park.

Walk 4
Llyn Trawsfynyd

*Trawsfynydd stands high above the Vale of Ffestiniog, the perfect spot
for the lake to be made into a reservoir for a hydroelectric scheme
in the 1920s. This is a circular trail right around the lake, on trails that are
well-made and easy to follow. With the wild Rhinogydd on one side
and the hills of the Migneint on the other, it is easy to forget the large
power station on the shore and enjoy the solitude and remoteness of this spot,
almost central to the Snowdonia National Park. There are dams to walk along,
ancient woods to admire, and even a café stop.*

Looking out over a moody Llyn Trawsfynydd

Start/finish	Car park in Trawsfynydd /// shells.postage.tarnished
Distance	12.5km (7¾ miles)
Ascent	100m
Time	3hr 15min
Terrain	Hard tracks and some roads
Maps	OS Explorer Map OL18 Harlech, Porthmadog & Bala/Y Bala
Access	Trawsfynydd is on the A470 south of the Vale of Ffestiniog. There is a free car park in the centre of the village, with public toilets. The postcode for the car park is LL41 4SB
Facilities	Shops and pub in Trawsfynydd. Café next to the lake at the power station.

From the car park in **Trawsfynydd** ('across the mountain'), head out to the road and turn left. Follow the road a short distance past the statue of Hedd Wyn and turn right down the road 'Cefn Gwyn', opposite the Cross Foxes inn. Turn right past the playground and then right down a track with a footpath sign.

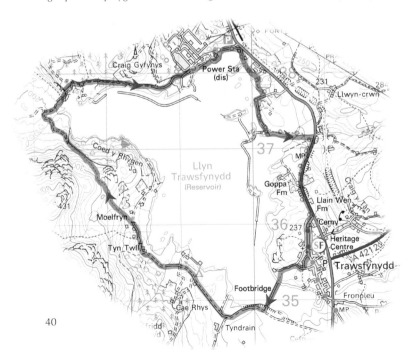

Crossing the footbridge over the narrowest part of the lake

Another track leads up a small outcrop, which reaches the war memorial and a view of the lake. Once on the track, continue until a footpath sign sends you left across a field and down to the long **footbridge** over **Llyn Trawsfynydd**.

Once over the bridge, drop down to the road and turn right. At the next road fork, turn right again to keep on the road that traverses round the western side of the lake.

At **Moelfryn** the road ends and three tarmac tracks lie ahead. Take the central track, marked with a footpath and cycle path sign, which bears left off the road. The other two tracks are private drives.

The track becomes a gravelled path uphill, recently built and easy to follow. As it heads downhill, the track passes the nature reserve and ancient woodland of **Coed y Rhygen**. Below this woodland on the right lies the northern edge of the lake. Follow the winding path all the way to the Maentwrog dam, ignoring a path that joins yours from the left as you approach the dam.

Although the nuclear power station on the northern shore of the lake is the most eye-catching, **Llyn Trawsfynydd** was converted into a reservoir for a wholly different power station. Sitting lower down in the valley near the village of Maentwrog is the hydroelectric power station, built in the 1920s and at the time able to provide electricity to the whole of North Wales. When the nuclear power station began using the lake water for cooling in the early 1960s there was a stipulation that the hydroelectric scheme could only use a certain amount of water, to guarantee the safety of the nuclear project. The hydroelectric power station still operates today, and the lake has become a popular site for fishing.

Cross the dam and continue on the track on the far side. This track continues for nearly 2km, under the slope of **Craig Gyfynys** and through woodland. On reaching the fence around the **power station**, continue ahead on the road until the lake appears on the right. Built in 1959, this is Britain's only inland nuclear power station. It is now being decommissioned, and the buildings slowly dismantled.

Head over to the concrete dam wall running along the lake when it appears, and follow the paved path alongside it. Ascend a small rise and go through a sheltered pavilion with information boards, and follow the path onwards to reach the car park for the **café** and fishing centre, which sits right on the lakeshore.

Go through the car park past the café and turn right to follow the track onwards, past the landing stage and into the woods. A path leads through these woods and comes to a gate, then a T-junction. Go through the gate and turn right to continue following the trail alongside the lake.

This track soon turns inland and crosses a stream to reach the road. On the road turn right and follow the pavement for around 1km until a sign points right indicating the entrance to **Trawsfynydd**. Follow this road into the village to return to the car park.

HEDD WYN

The statue of the war poet Hedd Wyn in Trawsfynydd

In the centre of the village stands the statue of Hedd Wyn, a war poet in World War 1 who lived and farmed nearby. He did not want to join up, but stepped in when his brother was conscripted, taking his place. He wrote several poems for local and national Welsh competitions and won the 1917 Eisteddfod with his poem *The Hero*, an anti-war poem. When it was revealed that he had won he was called forward to collect his prize, the famous bard's chair, only for the Eisteddfod to discover that he had just been killed in Flanders. The empty chair was then draped in black.

Unusually for someone killed in war, his statue depicts him as a shepherd rather than in uniform. You can visit and take a tour of his house, which has been restored, at Yr Ysgwrn, just outside Trawsfynydd (www.yrysgwrn.com).

Walk 5
Harlech

This walk is a wander around the countryside local to Harlech town and castle. Visiting the woodlands that cling to slopes just a short walk from the houses, it then heads up across farmland for views of the Rhinogydd, mountains that gaze over this part of the coast. Leading down to the coast itself the walk continues with a stroll along the beach and the sand dunes, with the Irish Sea and the Llyn Peninsula as a backdrop. The final stretch back to the castle is up what was for some time declared the steepest street in the world!

Harlech Castle, with the sand dunes and the Llŷn Peninsula in the distance

Start/finish	Harlech Castle gift shop /// airstrip.crumples.grab
Distance	8.8km (5½ miles)
Ascent	200m
Time	2hr 30min
Terrain	Farmland paths, tarmac and sandy beach
Maps	OS Explorer Map OL18 Harlech, Porthmadog & Bala/Y Bala
Access	Harlech is a major town and has ample car parking. The long stay car park can be found at LL46 2SR. The castle gift shop is next to the castle.
Facilities	Harlech has plenty of shops, pubs and cafés.

From the castle gift shop in **Harlech**, walk straight through the car park and take the path on the left-hand side under the bridge, then turn right. Pass the playground, and at the road turn left, downhill. After 50m turn right onto the track.

HARLECH CASTLE

After the English invasion of Wales at the end of the 13th century, led by Edward I and driven by the activities of Llywelyn the Last, Edward decided that North Wales had to be fortified against further revolt. Supplied by sea, which used to run right up to the castle rock, Harlech took only seven years to complete under the management of James of Saint George, and was ready in 1289 just in time for the revolt and siege of Madog ap Llywelyn in 1294–5.

Barely 100 years after its construction, in 1404 the castle was seized by the Welsh under Owain Glyndŵr during his rebellion, and became his home and the seat of the revolt for more than four years, being taken back in 1409. Later it played a key role in the Wars of the Roses: it was the last major fortification to be occupied by the Lancastrians and only taken in a massive siege in 1468 where the defenders faced insurmountable odds, giving rise to the song 'Men of Harlech'. In the English Civil War of the 17th century, it was held by the Royalists, and was the last castle to fall to the Parliamentarians in 1647. At the end of the war it was ordered to be demolished, an order that was only partially carried out.

Today, recognised by UNESCO alongside Edward I's other castles and fortifications in North Wales, Harlech is protected as a tourist attraction, and one of the finest examples of medieval military engineering in Europe.

At the start of the steps up to the road, turn left through a gate and follow the path through the woods. At the fork a few metres after a bench, take the left option, downhill. Follow the path on, across a bridge, to a T-junction, and turn right. Follow this path, which soon leads steeply uphill and reaches the road.

Cross straight over onto a track uphill, head up to a junction and turn right (straight ahead). After 400m join a track and continue ahead. Pass a chapel and reach a tarmac track fork by a parking spot for a graveyard. Take the left-hand option. On reaching the road a short distance away, turn left then after 30m turn right onto a footpath. Cross the stream and follow the path ahead, uphill.

The path starts well-defined but the most obvious trail soon leads the wrong way. As the path levels out, look out for two large piles of rocks, one on either side of the path. Head over to a single oak tree by the wall on the left, where stone steps lead across the wall. Cross these steps and head across the field towards the left-hand side of a ruined building.

Beyond the ruin follow the rough path uphill to a wall corner and cross it via another set of stone steps. Cross the field ahead keeping the wall on the right. There is another set of steps over the next wall, and then continue with the wall on the right. When the wall turns right, continue ahead up to the next wall and head right to find the crossing place in the corner. Continue up the next field as before; there is a yellow footpath arrow at the next crossing.

In the next field, head straight uphill. Find a gap in the wall and continue ahead on a pathless hillside. Aim for the stone wall on the top of the rise ahead; reach it and follow it right, past a gate and a corner, to a stone crossing with a yellow arrow. Cross this and go ahead to reach the road. The view ahead stretches over the Rhinogydd, the rough mountains at the heart of the National Park that include the oldest rock in Snowdonia, dating back to the Cambrian period.

At the top of the fields, the mountains of Rhinogydd come into view

Turn right on the road and follow it for 800m. At a junction, with a cattle grid and a footpath post on the left just before the 30mph zone, turn left onto the track. Only a few metres beyond the cattle grid, go right onto a footpath. After 150m go through the gate and turn right to head diagonally through the field, passing to the right of the telegraph pole and the pile of rocks. At the far side head through a gate and go down the next field, keeping the wall on the left. At the bottom of this field go ahead through a gate to follow a path between two walls.

Follow the right-hand wall to continue on the path, down to a tarmac track. Turn right, and at the road junction cross straight over and continue on, in the outskirts of **Llanfair**. After 100m turn right down Cae Garw. Continue ahead on the track and shortly take the path on the left between two fences. Go down the steps to the road, continue ahead and after 50m cross the road and go down the footpath.

The path is steep, with views of Harlech Cliff on the left; at the junction turn right and descend, crossing the railway to reach the beach. Turn right to walk along the beach, though it is also possible to walk through the sand dunes. In spring and early summer you can find flowers among the dunes and breeding birds searching for food. In winter there are plenty of waders, such as oyster-catchers, out on the sands.

After around 2km, a red-and-white post appears with a life ring. Head right here onto a path through the sand dunes. This soon becomes a hard path and leads through a **golf course**. At the road, go ahead. On reaching the T-junction

The beautiful sands of Harlech beach, flanked by mountains and sand dunes

with the main road, turn left, and then turn right down the tarmac with a footpath sign next to the sign for the railway station. At the **station**, go ahead through a gate in the white fence to cross the railway to a road.

Turn left on the road, pass a small **caravan park** and take the next road on the right. Follow this street uphill to a road junction by the shop at the top. This street is Ffordd Pen Llech, which at 37.45% was for some time declared the steepest street in the world, taking the title from a street in New Zealand. Unfortunately the criteria for measuring this record changed, and the New Zealand street regained the title. Turn right here to return to the castle gift shop.

Walk 6
Llanbedr

The landscape around Llanbedr is one of woodlands and low hills making their way from the mighty Rhinogydd Mountains to the sea. This walk weaves a line through this landscape, exploring two ancient woodlands, finding viewpoints up to the hills, and venturing through farmland. These lands are the watershed of the Afon Artro and the major coastal feature here is the river's estuary, visible from the hills as it enters the sea. There is an optional extension for walkers who want to visit the Nantcol Waterfalls.

Following a path next to the Afon Artro

Start/finish	The Victoria Inn, Llanbedr /// fearfully.blows.heads
Distance	8km (5 miles)
Ascent	200m
Time	2hr 30min
Terrain	Forest and farmland paths
Maps	OS Explorer Map OL18 Harlech, Porthmadog & Bala/Y Bala
Access	Llanbedr lies on the A496 coast road south of Harlech. There is on-street parking and a toilet block on the same street as the pub. Postcode is LL45 2LD.
Facilities	Llanbedr has a pub and café.

From the Victoria Inn in **Llanbedr**, cross the road bridge over the river and turn left immediately after onto a footpath. Continue ahead onto grass, staying to the left of the playground and sports field and following the hedge to a gate. Though the modern town of Llanbedr was built up around the slate industry, the area has been settled for thousands of years, as evidenced by nearby Neolithic standing stones.

Go through the gate and turn right, following the fence to a track. Follow this track on, and as it bends left through a gate, then past houses. At the junction with

The road through the woods above the Afon Artro

49

a tarmac track, turn left. This leads through woods, with the river on the left. At a track fork after 200m, go left, and shortly after the track crosses a stream, turn right off the track onto a footpath, where there is a metal post. The path runs up to another track; turn left here.

After 100m, pass a house and just afterwards, turn left at the fork. Go through the gate with the Woodland Trust sign for **Coed Aber Artro** and at the fork 50m later, go left. Follow this path and take the right-hand option at the fork by the small wooden post. This path reaches another fork beside a small stream; take the right-hand option, which leads straight on. This woodland is an ancient woodland, mainly consisting of oak and introduced beech, and is a fantastic spot for spring bluebells.

Cross over the road and continue on the path opposite, soon seeing the lake (actually a **reservoir**) on the left down the slope. The path leads gradually down to a **footbridge** over the Afon Cwmnantcol. Cross this and follow the faint path ahead diagonally right to where a tarmac track goes through a stone wall.

Optional extension to Nantcol Waterfalls (30min)

Turning right here onto the tarmac track takes you into a campsite. Take the first track on the right (there is a charge to access the walks here, which can be paid at reception). Follow the track next to the Afon Cwmnantcol, then when it vanishes continue ahead to join a path that follows the river past the **waterfalls**.

There are lots of trails, but stay next to the river and eventually pick up the blue-topped posts. This leads in a loop back to the campsite, with views over the Rhinogydd and the surrounding woodland, as well as other small waterfalls. Or it is easy to cut it short and just head back to the entrance at any point via the network of paths.

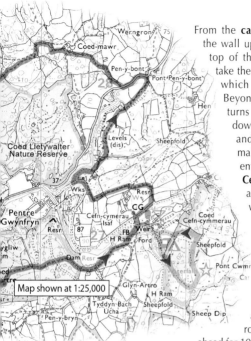

Map shown at 1:25,000

From the **campsite entrance**, follow the wall uphill. On the road at the top of the slope, turn right, and take the next footpath on the left, which runs in-between walls. Beyond another gate, the wall turns left after 50m. Follow it down, crossing a ruined wall and continue following the main wall. Shortly before the entrance to the farmyard at **Cefn-cymerau Isaf**, turn right and follow the wall on, which soon bends left.

After 200m, go through the gate ahead and continue down to another gate 100m away. Do not go through it but follow the path as it bends right and leads ahead to the road. On the road, turn right. Continue ahead for 100m past the house and the graveyard. At the start of a stone wall on the right, turn right onto a path towards the Afon Artro through trees. The path almost immediately bends right to reach the river. Follow the riverside path upstream (keeping the river on the left).

The path rises up, passes through a gate and follows an old wall. Once through another gate, the path heads up to an open area and bends left (ignore the faint path on the right). Head for 300m across the open area on the grassy path. On reaching a gate, go through it onto a grass and earth track. Follow this ahead for 200m.

At the junction with another track, go left and cross the bridge at **Pont Pen-y-bont**. Turn left on the road, and after 150m turn right onto a track. Follow this 300m up to **Coed-mawr**, passing a pond to reach a gate. Go through the gate (or via the stone steps), then almost immediately turn left at the yellow arrow, following the path into the trees and through a gate.

Immediately after the gate, turn right at the fork and follow the path steeply up above the house and then round following the wall/fence. Cross the stile and

A stream descends into the Afon Artro

turn left, following the fence. The path goes through the woods, then a semi-open area, then woods again. At the fork, go left, downhill; soon follow the old stone wall to the gate to enter **Coed Lletywalter**, a woodland owned by the Woodland Trust.

Soon go through two gates 100m apart, leaving the woodland. Go ahead, following the wall uphill. On reaching a track after 200m, turn left, and at the fork after 100m, take the left-hand option. With views now over the hills, at the next junction turn right, back uphill.

Pass a small house, and at the fork next to the farm at **Penrallt** before the cattle grid, take the right-hand option to pass the farm. At the next fork, where the right-hand option leads towards the house, go straight ahead. Go through the gate and continue ahead, following the wall. The path descends, with a view over the sea and the estuary of the Afon Artro.

The **estuary** as you see it now is actually further north that it has been. In 1819 it was diverted to its current position to allow better access to the wharf at Pensarn, where slate was shipped. It used to enter the sea south of Mochras (Shell Island).

Ignore the first footpath post and continue on, following the path as it bends left downhill through a gate. Follow it down through the woods and turn left on the road. At the main road, turn right to return to Llanbedr and the Victoria Inn.

The trail leads through the woods of Coed Aber Artro

Walk 7
Black Falls

This walk explores the forest around the hamlet of Ganllwyd in the old Dolmelynllyn Estate, nestled in the heart of Coed y Brenin. The first stop after a stroll up the Afon Gamlan is the Black Falls, a pair waterfalls that plunge 18m into a swirling pool. The trail then leads up into the forest and rewards you with views out into Cwm Camlan and the Rhinogydd before traversing the hillside to visit the ruins of the Cefn Coch gold mine. It then descends through oak woodland to return you to the valley.

Coed y Brenin and Rhobell Fawr on the wide view from Cefn Coch gold mine

Start/finish	Ganllwyd National Trust car park /// hawks.assume.mocking
Distance	6km (3¾ miles)
Ascent	220m
Time	2hr
Terrain	Forest tracks and paths
Maps	OS Explorer Map OL18 Harlech, Porthmadog & Bala/Y Bala
Access	Ganllwyd is on the A470 north of Dolgellau and the car park is sign-posted next to the main road in the centre of the hamlet. Postcode is LL40 2HE.
Facilities	None on the walk, other than a toilet at the car park. Nearest shops/ refreshments are in Dolgellau.
Note	There is an information board in the carpark detailing a few shorter walks, lasting from 1–4 hours.

From the National Trust car park in **Ganllwyd**, labelled as Dolmelynllyn, head to the road and turn left; then cross the road and take the first right, after the black-and-white hall. Head up the tarmac track with the Afon Gamlan on the left.

At the fork, take the left option towards the **Rhaeadr Ddu**. The track does not run right next to the river, so as it bends left, head off the track onto rough paths to hug the riverside as you head upwards, giving a better view of the small rapids.

At the footbridge, cross over and turn right to follow the path up to view-points over the **Black Waterfalls**, which has two stages. After viewing the falls, return to and cross the footbridge again, and follow the path ahead to a T-junction with the track. Turn left here, and after 100m, turn left up a joining track. This track soon passes through a gate and follows a wall uphill.

Although many of the hillsides are now used for **conifer plantations**, the woods used to be managed for their oaks. The wood was used for housing and shipbuilding on the Mawddach, and the bark was used in tanneries.

55

The Black Falls cascade down several steps into the dark pools below

Becoming a path, the route passes a house at Tyddyn-y-bwlch on the left-hand side and runs between two walls. On reaching a gate, go through it and join the track ahead, to continue in the same direction. At a T-junction after 200m, turn left, and then after 400m at a track fork, take the left option, staying closer to the river. After 100m, turn left to cross the bridge over the river, then at the fork straight after, take the right option. Views open up on the right over Cwm Camlan and the Rhinogydd, the oldest rocks in Snowdonia.

After 500m along this track, a crossroads of paths is reached. Look out for it, as the paths are smaller than the track you're currently on. At this crossroads, turn left onto the path.

This path eventually leaves the forest, giving views down over the forest and to Rhobell Fawr. It continues traversing the slope until reaching a cattle grid. Pass by this grid and continue along the track to the right of the barn. This track soon crosses another cattle grid and enters the forest.

Follow this track for 500m. As the track bends hard left, turn right, uphill, onto a joining track, where there is a green arrow on a post. After 50m, turn left to cross a stile and a footbridge over a stream, and follow the path ahead uphill, past the sign pointing towards Cefn Coch. The path becomes indistinct, but follow it up to a clear grassy track, and turn left to arrive at the ruins of the **gold mine**.

The ruins of the Cefn Coch gold mine on the slopes of Y Garn

Cefn Coch is just one gold mine in an area that saw a substantial gold rush in the second half of the 19th century, earning it the nickname 'New California'. Welsh gold is famously used in royal wedding rings, a practice that continues to this day, even if it makes up just 1% of the ring.

Continue ahead on the grassy level track past the old mine buildings, for around 200m round the bend. Beside a small ruin, turn left at a footpath post, downhill through a gate. The grassy path down is distinct, soon crosses a high stile and continues ahead to the left of a ruin, and then straight on to a stile/gate ahead.

Following the trail through the woods above the Afon Gamlan

Beyond the stile cross straight over the tarmac track, near Berth-Lŵyd, and follow the track ahead to cross a footbridge into the woods of Coed Ganllwyd, part of the **Dolmelynllyn estate**. Beyond the bridge turn right and follow the path ahead, downhill. At the crossroads, continue ahead, soon reaching the Afon Gamlan. Cross the stile and head down the field to reach the road. Turn left to return to the National Trust car park.

Walk 8
Pistyll Cain

This walk through forest and along the Mawddach River is an easy way into the heart of Coed y Brenin, to see the impressive waterfall of Pistyll Cain. Plunging 20m off a rock slab, it has been a popular beauty spot since the Victorians began visiting the area. The walk is along forest tracks and is easy to follow, also visiting the nearby waterfall of Rhaeadr Mawddach, before continuing the loop through the woods back to the car park.

Pistyll Cain on the Afon Gain surrounded by Coed y Brenin

Start/finish	Tyddyn Gwladys car park in Coed y Brenin /// radiated.emerald.lands
Distance	3km (1¾ miles)
Ascent	50m
Time	1hr
Terrain	Forest tracks
Maps	OS Explorer Map OL18 Harlech, Porthmadog & Bala/Y Bala
Access	From the hamlet of Ganllwyd, take the minor road which leaves the A470 next to the national speed limit signs to the north of the village. Follow this road for a few miles until it ends at the Tyddyn Gwladys car park. Rough postcode is LL40 2HS.
Facilities	None on walk. Café at Coed y Brenin visitor centre and more facilities in Dolgellau.

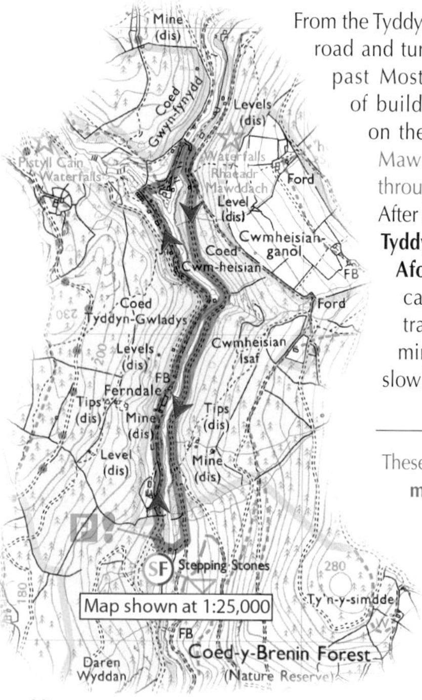

From the Tyddyn Gwladys **car park**, go back to the road and turn right. Follow the track onwards past Mostyn Cottage and at the next set of buildings take the track to pass them on the left. This track follows the Afon Mawddach, which you can see down through the trees, creating the gorge.

After around 1km, passing through **Coed Tyddyn-Gwladys**, the confluence of the **Afon Mawddach** and the **Afon Gain** can be seen below. Also along the track are numerous remains of old mining buildings, which can be seen slowly being taken over by vegetation.

These buildings form part of an **old gold mine**, built during the gold rush in the area in the second half of the 19th century. Besides gold, copper and manganese were also mined in the forest.

The Afon Mawddach begins to gorge up as it cuts through the rock below

Cross the bridge, where the view left is up to the 20m high waterfall at **Pistyll Cain**. Once over the bridge there is an out-and-back path on the left-hand side to get closer to the waterfall.

Once back on the track, continue ahead, taking the left-hand option at a fork after 50m. Pass the hydroelectric works and enjoy the view of the **Rhaeadr Mawddach**, also an impressive waterfall.

Started in the 1920s, the plantation forest surrounding this walk is part of a large forest called **Coed y Brenin**. The name, meaning the 'King's Forest', comes from 1935, when one forest in each of England, Scotland and Wales was re-named the King's Forest in honour of King George V's Silver Jubilee. Initially, it had been called Vaughan Forest after the main landowner, head of the Nannau Estate, whose history dates back to the 1100s. Originally planted by the Forestry Commission, it is now owned by Natural Resources Wales and is a major mountain bike and trail running centre.

Continue for 100m, and at the crossroads in **Coed Gwyn-fynydd**, turn right on the track to cross the bridge. Follow the track as it bends right and at the junction after 100m, take the right option, downhill through **Coed Cwm-heisian**.

After around 800m on this track, go right at a fork, downhill. Pass a few streams and you'll soon see the car park over the river on the right. There is a path going right, down to the river next to a bike track post. This leads to some **stepping stones** over the river and back to the car park.

However, if the river is high they can easily be underwater; in this case, continue along the track and take the next path on the right, by a yellow-topped post. This leads to a bridge over the river. At the path fork on the other side, take the right-hand option to return to the car park.

THE MAWDDACH ESTUARY

The wetland next to the estuary during a very high tide! (Walk 14)

Walk 9
Barmouth

*Sitting at the mouth of the Afon Mawddach with pristine beaches and a
beautiful dune system, Barmouth is one of Wales' true seaside resorts.
This walk starts in the town and leads up to the hillside of Dinas Oleu
before taking a meandering balcony route across low hills and upland farms
with fantastic views down over the coast and across the bay to the Llŷn
Peninsula and Bardsey Island. Descending to the 13th-century church at
Llanaber, it then joins the coast and returns to Barmouth along the beach,
always with the sound of the sea close by.*

Looking down over Barmouth and the mouth of the Mawddach Estuary from Dinas Oleu

Start/finish	Barmouth Lifeboat station /// contain.wove.forgiven
Distance	9km (5½ miles)
Ascent	340m
Time	3hr
Terrain	Upland paths and beach
Maps	OS Explorer Map OL18 Harlech, Porthmadog & Bala/Y Bala
Access	The major car park in Barmouth is on the coast road at LL42 1NF, and the lifeboat station is next to the car park.
Facilities	Barmouth has shops, cafés and pubs.

From the lifeboat station in **Barmouth/Abermaw**, face the sea and head left along the promenade. Follow the road left at the estuary mouth past the dolphin statue. The bridge over the estuary appears ahead as the road passes the **harbour**. Follow the road under the railway bridge and turn right at the junction.

Follow this road for around 200m, and as it bends right uphill, turn left onto a signed footpath next to a bench, up steep stairs. Pass the National Trust sign announcing your entrance to Cae Fadog, and soon after this the path becomes grassy and you are con-fronted by a large cliff.

Turn right, and take the right path option fol-lowing the dark green arrow, uphill. The path goes around the hill-side to give a panorama of the estuary, passing sev-eral benches. It descends and joins another path, and heads up steps between stone walls with a house on the right. Shortly after this, when still next to the house, turn left at a path junction. Soon this path arrives at a wall, with a gate on the right.

Barmouth and Dinas Oleu from the beach

Continue ahead to explore the summit of **Dinas Oleu**, and then return to this point. In 1895, this small hilltop, whose name means 'fort of light', became the first property to be given to the National Trust, which was formed the same year. It was previously owned by landowner and philanthropist Fanny Talbot, who donated it because she wanted it 'secure for the public forever'. The National Trust is now one of the largest private landowners in the UK, whose task is to protect sites for future generations.

Go through the gate and turn left on the path on the far side. Follow the path ahead, which leads down to a wall corner with a gate. Along this route is a detour on the left down to the Frenchman's Grave. This can be explored before returning to the route.

Go through the gate and turn right, uphill. At a junction after 100m, turn right and continue zig-zagging uphill. When a circular stone enclosure appears on the right, go up past it and through the gate in the wall on the other side. A few metres beyond the gate turn left on the path and follow it as it hugs the hillside, with Barmouth below. Ahead over the waters of Tremadog Bay the hills of the Llŷn Peninsula and Bardsey Island over on the left are easily visible on a good day.

After 200m at a junction with a path next to a footpath post, turn right, uphill. After 500m, you'll reach the ruined mine buildings at Cell-fechan. Continue

The mine ruins at Cell-fechan on the way up the hillside

ahead; the path winds uphill, where there are footpath posts and a sign for the Taith Ardudwy Way. The path runs straight, to the right of a ruined wall, and soon drops down towards a small valley.

At the junction here turn right, after 100m pass through a gap in a stone wall, and 50m further on turn left onto a path towards a house at **Gellfawr**. The path crosses a stream and then runs next to a fence all the way to the house. When directly in front of the house, turn left onto a clear footpath, which leads around the hillside.

After around 200m, on reaching what feels like a fork, go left on the path between walls, following a yellow arrow. At another fork soon after, go right uphill and through a gate. On the hillside below the stone walls wind around natural features in a sinuous series of field boundaries that never seem to end.

The path flattens out as it heads through **Ffridd y Graig** and passes through a gate in a stone wall beneath **Bwlch y Llan**. At the junction immediately after take the left-hand option to continue round the hillside above the sea.

On crossing another gate/stile, the path starts descending as it passes through Ffridd Fechan. Look out on the right-hand side for a ring of rubble on a low mound. This is an ancient settlement, probably an Iron Age fort.

The path descends for around 500m before following a wall to a gate. Go through the gate and immediately turn left through another gate to follow the path ahead downhill between walls. The path enters a field but is reasonably clear, and just continues ahead.

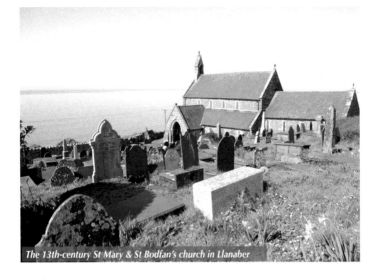

The 13th-century St Mary & St Bodfan's church in Llanaber

In the next field **Llanaber** and the church appear below. An obvious path heads down diagonally and then straight down between walls towards the church.

On reaching the track outside the house, turn left through a gate onto tarmac and follow it down to the main road. Turn left here and pass **St Mary and St Bodfan's Church**.

St Bodfan was a Celtic missionary from Bardsey Island who founded a church here in the 6th century. Though none of that building exists today, the current church dates back to the 13th century and is now a Grade 1 listed building. Inside the church there is a detailed guide to the building, which takes you round the points of interest.

Towards the end of the cemetery turn right at a footpath sign to follow a path down to a bridge over the railway line. Descend the steps and head along the sea wall towards Barmouth, with the sea on the right.

At the end of the concrete wall, continue along the fence. It is possible to choose between the promenade and the beach in order to follow the coast back towards central Barmouth. This leads back to the lifeboat station, past the dunes.

Walk 10
Mawddach to Ysgethin

This linear walk leads up and over the flanks of the Rhinogydd on the old droving road from Bontddu and the Afon Mawddach, to the coastal plain in Dyffryn Ardudwy. It is a landscape that has been lived in for thousands of years, shown by the Bronze Age cairn on the summit of the pass. It was on this trail during the Middle Ages that the main route from the coast ran, and where drovers would herd cows, sheep and geese to market. It also starts and finishes along paths through wooded streamsides, hidden worlds from the moorland and mountains above.

The trail heads across the cwm of the Afon Dwynant

From the Fiddler's Elbow car park at the eastern end of Bontddu, cross the main road to a layby and turn left. Take the next left down a track to **Rhuddallt**.

Head through the yard and follow the yellow arrow through a gate on a path to the riverside. Turn right and follow the riverside path. This sandy river estuary is the Afon Mawddach, and the river expands and contracts a huge amount with the tide.

The path becomes a track and soon bends inland to a gate. Turn left here, following the footpath sign to stay next to the river. Follow the path past a woodland and reach a track beside a water treatment site. Follow the track along the stream, and when the track bends right, go off the track to follow the path along the fence. This leads to tarmac; follow it up to the road through **Bontddu**. Cross the road and turn left.

Start	Fiddler's Elbow car park in Bontddu /// acids.refers.surface
Finish	A496 in Tal-y-bont /// private.towel.softly
Distance	12.5km (7¾ miles)
Ascent	500m
Time	4hr
Terrain	Hill paths and tracks, with some woodland
Maps	OS Explorer Map OL18 Harlech, Porthmadog & Bala/Y Bala
Access	Bontddu is on the A496 a few miles west of Dolgellau and the Fiddler's Elbow car park is on the right just before entering the 30mph zone from this direction, roughly at LL40 2UG. Tal-y-bont is also on the A496, a few miles north of Barmouth. There is a small car park just off the main road at LL43 2AN.
Facilities	Pub and restaurant in Tal-y-bont. Nothing in Bontddu.
Note	Bus number 39 runs between the start and finish points. For a timetable please see www.traveline.cymru

Bontddu is situated where the Afon Cwm-llechen meets the Afon Mawddach and used to be where the main road went inland rather than continuing along the coast to Barmouth as it does today. The site of the Clogau gold mine sits in the trees above the village, and it is this mine that provides the gold for royal wedding rings.

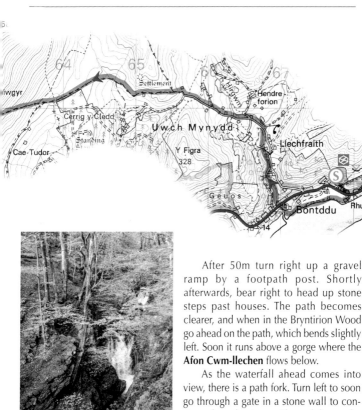

After 50m turn right up a gravel ramp by a footpath post. Shortly afterwards, bear right to head up stone steps past houses. The path becomes clearer, and when in the Bryntirion Wood go ahead on the path, which bends slightly left. Soon it runs above a gorge where the **Afon Cwm-llechen** flows below.

As the waterfall ahead comes into view, there is a path fork. Turn left to soon go through a gate in a stone wall to continue along the stream. The path leaves the

Following the Afon Cwm-llechen up past waterfalls

71

stream but still runs parallel, up to reach a hut by a bridge. Continue past the hut uphill, still on the right of the stream.

The path becomes a track; follow it roughly 700m all the way up to the road near Ty-glan-afon. Turn left on the road and follow it nearly 1.5km to where it ends at a track and path junction, at Banc-y-Frân. Take the right-hand path through the gate; it leads steeply up and reaches a path fork. The view right here reaches up to the southern Rhinogydd, the highest peak here being Diffwys (750m).

Take the left-hand option. From here the path is easy to follow, through the cwm to cross the Afon Dwynant and then runs next to a forest, now more like a track. After the forest follow the track through two more gates. Immediately after the second gate turn right towards a gate; before reaching this gate turn left onto a path that comes into view running diagonally downhill.

Follow this path all the way up to the 450m pass of the **Bwlch y Rhiwgyr**, where the sea and the Llyn Peninsula come into view ahead, and closer at hand the landscape of Dyffryn Ardudwy.

Bwlch y Rhiwgyr is known as the pass of the drovers, as it was a key droving route used to move livestock south from the plains around Harlech, from the Middle Ages onwards.

Crossing Pont Fadog over the Avon Ysgethin

Continue ahead downhill after the gate and the Bronze Age **cairn**. Go through the next gate you come to and continue ahead downhill. On reaching another gate, go through it and follow the path ahead along the wall. Look out for the remains of Neolithic stone circles over the wall on the left-hand side.

After around 1.5km, cross the gate/stile and continue straight ahead across the open area, on what is a grassy path. Pass through another gate/stile and the path now heads downhill towards a wooded valley, the valley of the **Afon Ysgethin**. After another gate, follow a concrete path onwards. Cross the 18th-century packhorse bridge at **Pont Fadog** and follow the track onwards.

At the first house, turn left onto a path. The path follows and leads down to the Afon Ysgethin, through the woods of Coed Cors-y-gedol.

At the fork take the left option to stay next to the river, and in general continue along the river, choosing each path option that keeps you closer to it. On arriving at the road and houses on the outskirts of **Tal-y-bont**, pass the Ysgethin pub (or go in!) and follow the track along the river to reach the main road. There is a bus stop, public toilets, and a pizzeria. The railway station is a short walk further on (turn left, then right).

The Afon Ysgethin, surrounded by perfect habitat for mosses and ferns

Walk 11
New Precipice Walk

Exploring the hillsides and woodlands where the Mawddach is joined by the Afon Cwm-mynach, the highlight of this walk is the incredible balcony path of the New Precipice Walk. This old tramway gives you views from Dolgallau right along the Afon Mawddach down to the sea, before the walk extends into the lower reaches of Cwm Mynach and explores the Nature Reserve of Coed Garth Gell, with its hidden gold mine remains.

The sun goes down over the Irish Sea from the New Precipice Walk

Start/finish	Car park just outside the entrance to Cymer Abbey, next to the River Mawddach /// archive.cube.afraid
Distance	12km (7½ miles)
Ascent	450m
Time	3hr 45min
Terrain	Mostly small paths, with some sections of track
Maps	OS Explorer Map OL18 Harlech, Porthmadog & Bala/Y Bala
Access	When driving between Dolgellau and Llanelltyd, turn down the road signposted to Cymer Abbey. There is a National Park car park just before the bridge (the old bridge), and a layby. The nearest postcode is LL40 2HE.
Facilities	None on the walk. Nearest shops/refreshments are in Dolgellau.

From the Cymer Abbey car park, exit the car park and turn right to follow the road across the old bridge over the **Afon Mawddach** ('little Mawdd river'). Beyond the bridge continue ahead up the path to the left of the small building towards **Llanelltyd** ('church of St Elltud'). Cross over the main road towards the bollards, pass between them, and bear left along the minor road.

Follow the road over the bridge. The road then bears right; follow it until the point where it nearly rejoins the main road. On the right, there is a footpath going uphill, beginning with three steps and signposted towards the 'New Precipice Walk'. Follow this path up into the forest.

At the first path fork, take the left route uphill, rather than the one which follows the wall. The path crosses a fence at a stile; go ahead and after 30m two paths appear on the right. Take the one that goes uphill. Shortly afterwards you will reach another fork; bear left and cross the wall over a stile to reach Llyn Tan-y-graig. Llyn Tan-y-graig

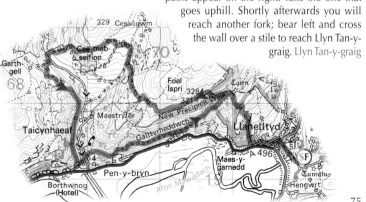

Llyn Tan-y-graig, an old reservoir just above Llanelltyd

is actually a reservoir, which once supplied drinking water to the village of Llanelltyd.

The path soon bends right and goes uphill between trees. At the next path junction marked by yellow arrows, continue ahead uphill. The path leads through woodland and reaches a wall.

Cross the wall via the stile and turn left, to pass the ruined house. The path continues, over a footbridge and past another ruined house. You are now on the **New Precipice Walk** and after heading uphill, you soon reach another wall crossing. This flat balcony path follows the line of an abandoned tramway, built to service the Voel gold mine, one of many gold mines in the area. About 500m further on, a white house comes into view ahead at Foel-Ispri-uchaf.

Follow the path as it leads to the left of the house, and past barns to the gate. Go through the gate onto the tarmac track and follow it as it winds downhill. After 300m, go through a gate and cross a small stream. Soon after, reach another gate and a large stream where the track bends left, uphill. 50m past the stream, turn right onto a track, uphill, where there is a sign for the farm Cesailgwm Mawr, and the stream is on the right.

The track swings left and reaches the farm buildings at Cesailgwm-mawr. Go through the first gate and then follow the yellow arrows round the left-hand side of the buildings. Cross a small stream, then keep the wall on the right and head up to the top corner of the field. Go through the gate, where there is a white arrow, then turn right on the track. After 50m, at a fork, take the left option to follow the track uphill to a building.

At the yard outside the building, go straight ahead through a few close gates to cross the stile ahead. Turn left and head up the path for around 10m until it disintegrates. At this point, follow the faint path that traverses the hillside, keeping at roughly the same level. Soon it passes a ruined wall.

After roughly 200m, when a forest appears ahead, head towards it, keeping in the same field, to reach the forest wall. Turn left to follow the wall down, past piles of rocks, and cross the stile to get into the forest. There is a footpath post straight after, inside the forest. Continue straight ahead, following the path and the fence. After passing a building at **Cae-mab-seifion**, the path becomes faint but heads steeply downhill. Keep the fence on the left. At the bottom, cross the stile and go through the gap in the wall ahead; turn right on the track.

On reaching the minor road, turn left, and then after 100m, turn right to cross the bridge over the **Afon Cwm-mynach**. Go through the gate, and turn left at the track fork. The track ascends, and levels out to pass above a house, then bends right and reaches a junction of paths. Turn left. Bear slightly left in the field to follow the rough grassy path ahead. On reaching a gate and a stile, cross the stile to enter the woodland and nature reserve of Coed Garth Gell, which is owned by the RSPB.

COED GARTH GELL

Coed Garth Gell is protected as a site of special scientific interest for its wild-life, especially small birds, mosses and lichens, which thrive in the damp gorge. The conditions make this a great example of a Celtic Rainforest, a habitat crucial for native species and which has suffered massive losses over the past few hundred years. Protecting areas like this is vital to conserve a unique habitat of the western British Isles.

On this trail down through the woods there are also many ruins from the old gold mine, including entrance shafts into the hillside and the foundations of buildings. Gold was first mined in the area by the Romans, but became more commercial in the second half of the 1800s, where a gold rush in the area led to the establishment of several mines. The last of these only closed in 1998, and there has even been recent prospecting to find a way of bringing out what gold is left. So yes, there is gold in them hills!

Follow the path ahead through the woodland for 1km, until houses appear ahead and the path reaches a gap in a stone wall. At this point, turn left downhill

Following the path through the forest at Galltyrheddwch

on an earthy path down to the river. Cross the bridge and follow the path up to the road near **Pen-y-bryn**. Turn left on the road, and after 50m turn right onto a path through trees, where there is a footpath sign.

Continue ahead for 100m to a fork, and take the right option through an old gate. The path continues through the forest for 300m following a mossy stone wall. On reaching a path fork, take the left option, uphill, where there is a yellow-topped post. At another fork after 50m, turn right following the white arrow. The path ascends and becomes quite rough but soon emerges onto a track running through **Galltyrheddwch**. Turn right.

After half a mile, when the track becomes tarmac and bends right, go ahead, and at the immediate path fork, take the left option uphill, which is steep at first and then levels out. The path steepens again while going up a small gully. At the top of the gully at a faint fork, take the right option, which continues straight ahead. On reaching two parallel fences, continue ahead.

Keep ahead, with a fence on the right, and cross the wooden footbridge over the stream. The path continues for around 100m but then disappears among the trees, with dense vegetation ahead. At this point, bear left uphill through the trees, keeping the steeper hillside on the left. There are frequent wooden posts with black-and-yellow tape. After around 150m uphill, the path becomes clearer again.

Continue ahead along a path that feels like a drainage ditch for another 150m to a path junction (a crossroads, with a footpath post). Turn right here and follow the path back down to Llyn Tan-y-graig. Go through the gate beyond the lake and at the fork after 20m, turn right. At the next fork, after 100m, take the left option and head towards the gate/stile. Cross the stile and follow the path ahead down-hill; retrace your steps through Llanelltyd to the Cymer Abbey car park. Cymer Abbey is an 11th-century Cistercian Abbey, built to control a ford over the Afon Mawddach. You can visit all year and entry is free.

Walk 12
Precipice Walk

Opened in 1890 by the local estate, the Precipice Walk has always been popular. With hardly any ascent and descent, it leads you round the flanks of Foel Cynwch, with fantastic views down the Mawddach and over Cadair Idris and the Rhinogydd. It is easy to walk and to navigate, and also includes a visit to the glistening waters of Llyn Cynwch. Although the sides of the hill are sometimes steep and you may want a small head for heights, the path is always clear. The summit of the hill, though not visited, is crowned by the Iron Age fort of Foel Faner, dating back to 800 years before the Roman invasion.

Looking out over the slopes of Foel Cynwch towards the Mawddach Estuary

Start/finish	Coed y Groes car park, north of Dolgellau /// unlisted.origin.spelled
Distance	5.5km (3¼ miles)
Ascent	50m
Time	1hr 30min
Terrain	Hillside paths
Maps	OS Explorer Map OL18 Harlech, Porthmadog & Bala/Y Bala
Access	Head north-east on the minor road that rises up out of Dolgellau opposite the bridge; continue following the road until you reach the car park at Coed y Groes. Postcode is LL40 2NG.
Facilities	None on the walk. Nearest shops/refreshments are in Dolgellau.

In the car park at Coed y Groes, head up to the top of the car park and take the path on the right, which stays right and goes behind the toilet block. The path bends left round the hillside and then bends right in front of a field. On reaching a house at Gwern-offeiriaid, the path bends left to pass to the left of the house.

This walk partly passes through the private land of the **Nannau Estate**, though the hill itself is open access land. The Nannau Estate was owned by two of the most powerful families in the area, the Nanneys and the Vaughans, who were the lords of the area for hundreds of years. The estate dates back to the 12th century, though the current house is Georgian. Situated just south of the car park, it was completed in 1796 and among other uses was a hospital in World War 1. The surrounding lands and deer park are still part of the estate, so there is a small chance certain paths can be closed.

Follow the path ahead to the slope of the hill **Foel Cynwch**, where the path divides. Bear right, up the slope to a wall corner and turn right to follow the wall. Follow this path, which is the **Precipice Walk**, level round the hillside for around 2.5km. There are some steep drops on the right during this section. There are fantastic views in all directions,

81

A well-earned rest stop on the southern edge of Foel Cynwch

from the slopes of Y Garn across the Afon Mawddach, to Cadair Idris in the south and down the estuary to the Irish Sea.

The path keeps bending left, passing several gates and walls, and after around 3km traversing the hill, reaches **Llyn Cynwch**. Drop down to the lake and meet a track at the edge; turn left. Follow this track alongside the lake and past the far end. Llyn Cynwch is a reservoir that provides drinking water for Dolgellau, and is also a popular fishing spot.

Beyond the lake continue ahead across open ground to meet a gate. Go through the gate and follow the path back to the car park the same way as at the start.

The trail drops down to the reserve of Llyn Cynwch

Walk 13
Foel Offrwm

Foel Offrwm ('the hill of sacrifice') is a low hill rising to the north of Dolgellau, in the Nannau Estate and home to several Iron Age structures on its summit. This walk takes an almost level path, which contours around the hill, starting from a high point so giving fantastic views out over Cadair Idris, the Wnion valley and the Aran range. It is easy to follow and to navigate and is the perfect introduction to the wide-ranging landscape of South Snowdonia.

View from the route of Coed y Brenin and the Rhinogydd

Start/finish	Coed y Groes car park, north of Dolgellau /// unlisted.origin.spelled
Distance	4km (2½ miles)
Ascent	100m
Time	1hr 15min
Terrain	Hillside paths
Maps	OS Explorer Map OL18 Harlech, Porthmadog & Bala/Y Bala
Access	Head north-east on the minor road which rises up out of Dolgellau opposite the bridge; continue following the road until you reach the car park at Coed y Groes. Postcode is LL40 2NG.
Facilities	None on the walk. Nearest shops/refreshments are in Dolgellau.

Head to the top of the car park (the end opposite the entrance) and turn left to cross the road towards the hill of **Foel Offrwm**.

At the path fork immediately after, take the right-hand option, which soon bends right. Follow the path through a gate and continue onwards on a well-laid path, made by the National Park Authority, above Nannau Home Farm. Enjoy the experience of walking through a set of large beech trees, a type of woodland not typical of Snowdonia.

On the southern side of Foel Offrwm the view reaches further east towards the Arans

With Cadair Idris visible ahead, the path bends left. Pass a bench and continue along the grass. Head up the wooden steps and continue ahead, following the fence. Pass through a gate after 50m and continue onwards, going through another gate through a stone wall shortly after.

HOWEL SELE

At the beginning of the 15th century the Lord of Nannau was a man named Howel Sele, who was the cousin of the famous Welsh independence leader Owain Glyndŵr. However, they were known as enemies, and during a hunt in the grounds at Nannau, Howel attempted to kill Glyndŵr with an arrow. He failed, and Glyndŵr responded by drawing his sword and killing Howel on the spot. Not wanting war between the families, he hid Howel's body inside an oak tree, a truth he only told to Howel's widow on his death.

Almost immediately, the ghost of Howel Sele began to haunt the local area, being spotted outside the house, on the flanks of Cadair Idris, and up here on Foel Offrwm. The tree itself became notorious as a haunted site, and there were even stories of the branches reaching down and strangling passers-by to death.

The path continues level, running round the hillside. After passing a small rock outcrop there is an open area with a vague path fork; take the left option to continue round the hillside. Ahead, the Aran range is visible, with the highest point, Aran Fawddwy, rising to over 900m.

The path keeps bending to the left, passing the forest of Coed Pant-ebolion. After the forest the path rises a bit and the views open up to the north over Snowdon and the Rhinogydd. Continue along the path as it bends left; pass through a wooden gate and follow the path down to a track. The track reaches the road, which you should cross to return to the car park.

Walk 14
The Mawddach Estuary

The Mawddach Estuary is quite simply one of the most beautiful places in the whole of the British Isles. A wide sandy snaking riverbed, surrounded by the majestic peaks of the Rhinogydd and Cadair Idris, making its way down to the sea surrounded by woodland and hosting a bunch of interesting wildlife. This walk makes its way along the Mawddach Trail, the old railway line that runs along the riverside, before heading up into the surrounding countryside to visit Lynnau Cregennen. It then heads back down for a final wander through the ancient Abergwynant Woods before finishing back at the pub. Ideal!

Gazing over the Afon Mawddach from the viewpoint in Abergwynant Woods

Start/finish	Penmaenpool, George III Inn /// guilty.printers.bandstand
Distance	18.5km (11½ miles)
Ascent	350m
Time	5hr 15min
Terrain	Mostly tracks, with some upland paths
Maps	OS Explorer Map OL18 Harlech, Porthmadog & Bala/Y Bala; OS Explorer Map OL23 Cadair Idris & Llyn Tegid
Access	Penmaenpool is a few miles west of Dolgellau on the A493; the car park is off the road on the right, and is signposted. Postcode is LL40 1YB.
Facilities	Pub and toilets next to the start. Other facilities in Dolgellau.

From the car park at **Penmaenpool Bridge**, head past the toll bridge and follow the road to the right of the George III pub. The **Afon Mawddach** is on the right. The wooden toll bridge was built in 1879 to replace the ferry, and is still in use today. Even car sat-navs recognise that you need to pay a toll!

Beyond the pub, continue ahead on the track. When the houses end, go through the gate and continue ahead on the Mawddach Trail, which is a disused

The Mawddach Trail is also popular with cyclists, and bikes can be hired in Dolgellau

railway track. From here the trail starts in
the woods, and heads out into marsh-
land and finally alongside the river
again as it heads towards the
sea. The famous writer
John Ruskin, more
often associated
with the Lake

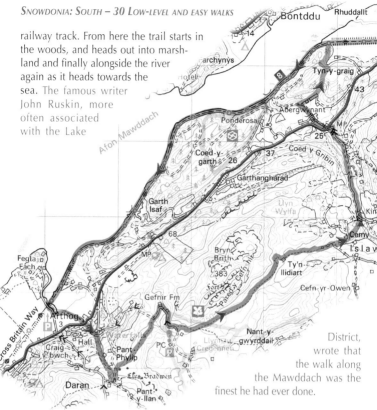

District,
wrote that
the walk along
the Mawddach was the
finest he had ever done.

Follow the trail for around 7km, until
it reaches **Arthog**, where the trail reaches a crossroads with a minor tarmac road
just after a stream bridge.

Turn left on the road. After 100m, turn left through a gate, where there is a
footpath sign. Follow the embankment path ahead. When the church and graveyard appear ahead after around 400m, at the end of the embankment, head 50m
across the field and go through a gate to the main road.

Turn left and walk up the road for 50m. Opposite the entrance to St Catherine's
Church, turn right onto a footpath. Follow the footpath up the steps ahead.

In another 10 minutes, once you reach a set of stone posts and a gate, continue ahead for 20m, then turn right onto a footpath with a yellow footpath arrow.
Continue following the path uphill, staying to the right of the stream. At the minor

waterfalls, the path zig-zags uphill. After crossing a stile over a stone wall, the path is then level.

The path crosses a few more stiles, still following the stream, then leaves the wood and joins a track, where a house is visible ahead. Almost immediately, turn left to cross a stone slab bridge over the Afon Arthog. Shortly after crossing the stream the path joins a track. On the right, the mountain of Cadair Idris comes into view, with its great north face a rampart of crags and gullies.

Turn left on the track, and at the track fork after the gate, continue ahead. 50m further on, go through another gate and then immediately take the faint

A stone slab bridge crosses the Afon Arthog

Llynnau Cregennen sits high in the foothills of Cadair Idris

path on the left, keeping the wall on the left. The distinctive summit of Pared y Cefn hir appears ahead; this hill has Iron Age settlements on its slopes.

Carry on for 150m then, when the wall bends left and there are two parallel walls, walk ahead across the field to a stile to the left of two large boulders, around 100m away.

Cross the stile and follow the path ahead, which stays level, following footpath signs. Soon cross the stone wall on the left via a stile and cross the field downhill to the road. Turn right on the road and follow it uphill for around 500m, passing **Gefnir Farm**. As the road crests a rise and the lake at **Llynnau Cregennen** appears ahead, turn left onto a footpath and head to a stile over a wall, with the lake on the right. At the fork after the stile, take the right-hand option. Follow the path ahead past the lake with the hill of **Pared y Cefn hir** on the left.

In another 1.5km, you'll reach a gate; go through it and follow the white arrows across the field ahead to a track at **Ty'n Llidiart**. On arriving at the track, continue ahead in the same direction. The track leads to a minor road; follow it ahead, with a small stream on the right.

As the road bends left round the ruined Methodist chapel and cemetery, turn right onto a footpath, where there is a footpath sign on a telegraph pole. Follow this path to another road and continue ahead on the road downhill.

Pass buildings at **YHA Kings** and continue ahead on the road, which soon follows the Gwynant stream. On reaching the main road, turn left and then immediately right onto a track towards **Abergwynant Farm**, which passes through an avenue of redwoods. After 200m, at the fork with a bridge on the left, take the right-hand option, which goes straight ahead.

In another 100m, at another fork, take the left option, then shortly after at another fork, take the right option and enter Abergwynant Woods. Once through the gate, turn right onto a path, which soon rises. When it flattens again, there is a footpath sign with three coloured arrows; turn right here onto a joining path, following the orange arrow.

The **Mawddach Estuary** is an important place for wildlife, especially birds such as waders, and the plants found in its woodland remnants. Shipbuilding used to be a major industry on the estuary, and Abergwynant Woods was one of the sources for the trees used to make the ships. Alongside gold mining, ship-building has sunk into history, and now the estuary provides a vibrant salmon and trout fishery alongside the other recreational uses for walking and cycling.

When you reach the path T-junction in 150m, turn right. Shortly the path reaches an out-and-back path to a viewpoint. Head the short distance to this viewpoint for a look over the Mawddach and then return to the junction to continue following the orange arrows. The path winds down and returns to the Mawddach Trail. Turn right here to return to Penmaenpool.

Walk 15

Morfa Mawddach and the Blue Lake

Beginning with a flat wander out along the very edge of the Mawddach Estuary to the sea, this walk starts easy, giving you a view of wild marshes and beautiful sandy beaches. After passing the crumbling World War 2 defences near Fairbourne it heads up to the Blue Lake and then joins upland paths and tracks for a panoramic tour above the valley, exploring the rolling moorland north of Cadair Idris. Heading back down through woodland, it finishes with a visit to the Arthog Bog Nature Reserve, a nationally important wetland site. This walk really has every type of lowland environment to explore.

**The wetlands where the Afon Mawddach meets the
sea with the Rhinogydd rising up behind**

Start/finish	Morfa Mawddach station car park /// chariots.beams.soil
Distance	13km (8 miles)
Ascent	360m
Time	4hr
Terrain	Mostly tracks, with some upland paths
Maps	OS Explorer Map OL23 Cadair Idris & Llyn Tegid
Access	Morfa Mawddach station car park (free) is signposted off the A493 just east of Fairbourne. Postcode is LL39 1BQ.
Facilities	Toilets at the car park. Café and shop in Fairbourne.

From the **Morfa Mawddach** station car park, go onto the platform and continue to the end, then through the gate onto the tarmac path. Barmouth and the estuary are visible ahead across the bridge.

After 50m turn left to cross the railway, and continue straight ahead towards Fairbourne. After roughly a mile, on reaching the road, instead of following the coast path left, go right for around 200m on the road until you can turn left, cross the miniature **Fairbourne Railway** and access the beach near **South Bank**.

Turn left and follow the beach past **Fairbourne**. At the far end of the beach, bear left to join the minor road and follow it through the tunnel under the main road. When the minor road joins the main road, continue ahead on the pavement, past **Friog Farm**.

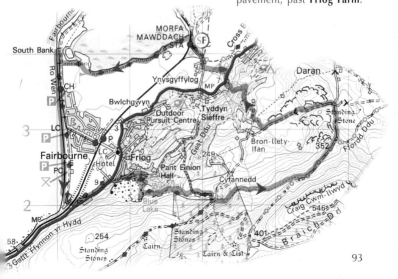

93

The World War 2 defences on Fairbourne beach, including the concrete 'Dragon's Teeth'

Look out for the World War 2 defences along the coastline here. There are several pillboxes, and a series of concrete 'tank traps' known as the Dragon's Teeth.

Continue for 500m, then turn right up the next street, Fordd Panteinion. After 400m, turn right through a gate onto a footpath, where there is a Coast Path sign. Follow this path, which winds steeply uphill alongside the remains of a disused Goleuwern slate quarry. As the path zig-zags up, follow the Coast Path signs. It is possible to explore a bit of the quarry off this track, including seeing an impressive set of winch wheels, and the view down to Fairbourne.

The Blue Lake sits in an old slate quarry high above Fairbourne

Eventually, the path takes you to a gate. Before going through this gate, take the dirt path on the right of the fence, uphill. This leads shortly to a grassy platform overlooking the **Blue Lake** and the quarry, and the view extends back down to Fairbourne and the sea. Take care as there is no fence before a large drop. After taking in the view, return down to the gate and go through it.

The **Blue Lake**, whose name needs no real explanation, is a famous spot, and was popular with wild swimmers and locals for many years afer the site, on private land, was opened up in the 1980s. The blue colour is due to copper sulphate from the surrounding rock, and on a sunny day you can see almost down to the bottom. It is of course artificial, sitting in a hole left by the slate mining activities of the site, which closed in the 1920s. Sadly in 2019, due to a huge increase in the amount of rubbish left at the site, the landowner blocked off the tunnel leading to the lake.

Carry on for 200m, then turn left onto the path downhill, which has been widened to track-width. Go through a gate and continue on the path, which bends right. The path crosses a bridge, and then a further stream. Soon after this it passes through a gap in a stone wall; go through it and turn right. The path heads up and bends to the left. Follow it past the left-hand side of a house at Cyfannedd-fawr and up to a road on a track.

At the road turn left, then immediately take the track on the right going diagonally uphill into the forest (not the track going straight uphill opposite the road). In 200m, when the track bends left at the edge of an open area, continue straight ahead on a grassy path going in the same direction as before. On reaching a stile over a fence, cross it and continue ahead on the path. It is overgrown but straight, and there is soon a wall on the right. Follow the trail onwards, through a gate and stile. The route is grassy but clear.

After the second gate, when the wall is now on the left, there is a plane crash memorial plaque on the wall. Shortly after this, the path joins a substantial track; continue ahead for 500m to a gate. There are great views on the left over Cwm pen llydan to the Mawddach Estuary and the sea.

Go through the gate, and 150m beyond it, as the track bends right, go straight ahead down a joining track, heading downhill. On reaching a crossroads with the road, turn left, uphill. Follow this road for just over 1km, and just before a stand of trees, before reaching **Bron-llety-ifan**, turn right onto a footpath, where there is a footpath post. Follow it over a footbridge and downhill. Follow the arrows to cross another bridge below a miniature hydroelectric weir.

Beyond the bridge, turn left and follow the arrows through two fields, then turn right towards a house. Half-way to the house, cross a stile and turn left to follow the wall and then fence downhill, where there is a great view of the Afon Mawddach Estuary and **Barmouth**.

Cross the stile at the bottom corner of the field and follow the path ahead through the woods. Cross another stile onto a tarmac track, and head downhill to the road, the A493. Turn right and follow the road for 50m before crossing it and turning left onto a path through the Arthog Bog Nature Reserve.

Arthog Bog is managed by the RSPB and is an important wetland habitat for all sorts of wildlife, especially insects and amphibians. This kind of lowland bog is quite rare, and you may see cattle and horses grazing to keep it open and stop scrub getting established. Look out here in the spring for specialised plants, including St John's Wort and yellow flag iris.

At the far end of the reserve, at the road, turn right and follow this road back to the station car park.

BALA TO DOLGELLAU

A path leading through the woods above Aber Gwenwyn-feirch (Walk 21)

Walk 16
Brithdir

This is a proper exploration of the landscape around the hamlet of Brithdir, nestled on the slopes above the Afon Wnion. Beginning by heading down the wooded gorge of the Afon Clywedog, the walk continues on forest trails along the valley floor, places where the spring bluebells are truly breathtaking. Then heading uphill, it joins tracks on the flanks of the western Aran mountains to look down on Brithdir and away over the hills to the north, before dropping back down again past the site of an old Roman fortlet.

The path through the woods of Coed Isaf, a beautiful place at any time of year

Start/finish	Layby on B4416 west of Brithdir before bridge and junction with A470 /// sliders.tarred.unstated
Distance	12km (7½ miles)
Ascent	450m
Time	4hr
Terrain	Woodland paths and tracks through the valley and along hillsides
Maps	OS Explorer Map OL23 Cadair Idris & Llyn Tegid
Access	To reach the start location from Dolgellau, drive south on the A470 and only a few miles out of town there is a turning left onto the B4416 to Brithdir. After the bridge the layby is clear on the left a few hundred metres later. A rough postcode is LL40 2RH.
Facilities	None on the walk. Nearest shops/refreshments are in Dolgellau.
Note	It is also possible to park in Brithdir village, opposite the village hall, and follow the route from where it passes this point (road junction in Brithdir), but there is less space for parking there.

Go through the gate at the start of the layby on the B4416 onto a path, which heads downhill, with the gorge and the Afon Clywedog on the left. Continue following the path; there are steps down after a few hundred metres. Follow the path for another 400m, where the path rises and a house can be seen ahead. The path meets a tarmac track. This section of the walk is also called the Torrent Walk due to the power of the river, especially in full flow. Visit after heavy rain for a real show!

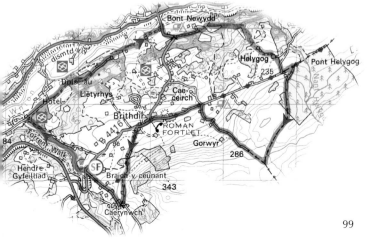

The path is easy to follow, past mosses and ancient trees above the Afon Clywedog

Turn left on the track, and then as it swings left, turn right onto a stony track down to a road in Coed Dôl-fawr and follow the road ahead. In 400m, as the road bends left at **Hotel**, go ahead through a gate onto a track near Cyfar Dolserau. Follow the track ahead for a few hundred metres through a gate into the forest of Coed Dolgwartheg at **Dolserau**.

At the track fork in the forest, take the left-hand option down towards the house. As the track bends left towards the house, continue straight ahead onto a footpath, where there is a yellow footpath arrow. Go through a gate and continue ahead on this path with a fence on the right.

Cross a footbridge over the stream and pass a ruin. The path becomes grassy in the next field; head straight across it and a gate appears ahead with a yellow arrow. Go through it and follow the frequent footpath posts ahead, crossing the next field with the river on the left. Pass through the gate and go ahead through the woodland.

Go straight ahead across the next field, keeping the fence on the left. Follow the arrows to a wooden gate. Beyond this gate go forward to a track and turn left. Shortly go through another gate and turn right over a concrete bridge to join a track near Felindre. Follow this track for 200m to the road.

Turn right on the road and follow it uphill. Take the first track on the left, after you've walked just over 200m. Follow this track 400m to a fork near Dol-gamedd. Take the right option and continue ahead. Go through the gate and along the track. Soon the track reaches a set of two gates. Go through the right-hand gate and then at the immediate fork, take the right-hand option, uphill, where the path feels like an old sunken track. At first keep the fence a short distance away on the right, then when the fence bends right keep on and upwards.

The path soon goes through a gate and rises up through the woodland of Coed Isaf. Cross the stile soon reached and enter the field, crossing it on the left-hand side to a gap on the far side. Beyond the gap, turn right. The path here pretty much disappears. Make your way uphill around the mossy boulders, keeping the stone wall approximately 50m away on the right. Continue up to a wall, and find the gap for the non-existent (though on the map!) footpath to pass through. Continue ahead through this gap.

The path is now clear again, and bears right, uphill, and soon reaches an old stony track. Turn left and follow the track for 100m. At the wall gap before the track enters a field, turn right and follow the mossy wall uphill. After 50m go through a gap in the wall and continue ahead. On reaching an open area, turn left, and look out for buildings ahead. Pass to the right-hand side of the buildings. Once past the buildings a track appears. Join the track and continue ahead. Follow it past the house at **Helygog** as it bends right, up to the road.

Turn right on the road. In 200m, as the road bends right, turn left through a gate onto a track, towards Pont Helygog. When you come to the junction in 150m, turn right uphill on a track that heads up and through a forest.

On reaching a gate at the end of the forest, head through it and continue along the track across the open fellside of Glasgwm. Pass through another gate

Descending along an upland track towards Brithdir with the Rhinogydd behind

in 200m, then continue. Shortly the track bends left and eventually points uphill, and you reach a junction. At this junction turn right, downhill on the earth track. This section provides fantastic views of the Mawddach Valley and the mountains of the Rhinogydd.

Soon, head through a gate, where the track continues between a wall and a fence. Follow it down, fording a small stream, where the track becomes tarmac shortly after. On reaching the road junction, turn left and follow the road. After entering the 30mph zone, there is a terrace of houses on the left at the start of **Brithdir**. After the wooden house on the right, there is a raised flat field on the right that was the site of a **Roman fortlet**.

BRITHDIR ROMAN FORTLET

Situated half-way between the fort at Tomen y Mur (Walk 3), and Pennal near Machynlleth, Brithdir was a smaller enclosure, possibly acting as a kind of police post. There are signs of several ditches, and possibly a bathhouse and workshops. Ceramic found on the site indicates it was in use from 125–45CE. Completely overgrown, it was only noticed during an aerial survey in 1961.

Follow the road through Brithdir to the road junction, and go left (straight on). When the pavement ends, turn left onto the dead-end road before the chapel, on the route of the Cross Britain Way. Follow it for 400m past the house at Ty'n-llidiart where it becomes a path. Head along the path and then through two gates, where the path then leads up over a grassy hillside. Ignore side paths and this path eventually runs in-between two walls, becomes a track and reaches a road at **Caerynwch**. Turn right and follow the road all the way down to the main road. The layby where the route started is on the right.

Walk 17
Foel Caerynwch

This small hill provides an excellent viewpoint over the valley around Brithdir, and away to the extinct volcano of Rhobell Fawr and the Rhinogydd, as well as back to the Aran range. The walk is short, leading up from the hamlet of Brithdir through fields and across moorland, and is mostly well signposted. After visiting the summit the descent is straightforward, also passing the site of Brithdir Roman Fortlet.

The moorland trail leading back into the Wnion valley and Brithdir

Start/finish	Brithdir village hall /// elbow.lunged.shun
Distance	3.4km (2¼ miles)
Ascent	170m
Time	1hr 15min
Terrain	Upland paths
Maps	OS Explorer Map OL23 Cadair Idris & Llyn Tegid
Access	Brithdir is signposted from the A470 and A494 just east of Dolgellau. At the road junction in the centre of the hamlet there is a village hall, opposite which there is some on-street parking at LL40 2RT.
Facilities	None. Nearest are in Dolgellau.

From the village hall in **Brithdir** go past the post box to the road junction and turn left (onwards) to follow the pavement on past the green bus stop. Just after the pavement ends, turn left onto a dead-end road, at the chapel, following the Cross Britain Way. The 279-mile Cross Britain Way is an alternative coast-to-coast, starting in Lincolnshire and ending just down the valley from here in Barmouth.

Pass the house at Ty'n-lliidiart after 500m and go onto the footpath ahead. Go through two gates and then follow the path ahead uphill. After 100m, turn left onto a path, still uphill. After going through a gate follow the wall ahead.

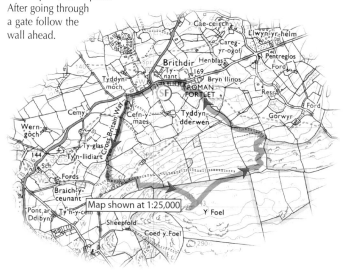

104

The valley of the Afon Wnion and the Rhinogydd from the ascent of Foel Caerynwch

At the wall corner, turn right, following the white arrows, and then follow the next arrow which sends you left, diagonally up. The path leads to the top wall and then along it to a stile. Cross the stile and follow the white arrow left. The path leads gradually uphill diagonally away from the wall. Continue following the white posts.

Follow the path to the summit of Foel Caerynwch (just called **Y Foel** on the OS 1:25,000 map), at 343m.

The view from the summit of **Foel Caerynwch** extends from the Mawddach Estuary over the Rhinogydd to Rhobell Fawr and the valley towards Bala. The Moelwynion are even visible in the distance in the north.

After visiting the summit, follow the continuation of the white posts, which heads downhill over moorland. Reach a wall and cross the stile when reached, then bear right to pick up the white posts again. Go through a gap in a ruined wall and continue on. At the next post there is a fork, take the left option, downhill. The path then zig-zags downhill, with intermittent posts, and is relatively straightforward to follow. It eventually leads down to a stile over a fence into a field.

Following the path back down towards Brithdir on the slopes of Glasgwm

Cross the stile and head down the field on the right-hand side to pass trees into another field. Continue on the right-hand side and at the bottom, continue ahead on the path towards the house. At the next yellow post, bear left and head across a small open area to the start of a stony track.

Follow the track between houses to reach the road and turn left here, passing the **Roman fortlet** in a field on the right, to return to Brithdir and the village hall. The Roman fortlet was the half-way stop between the larger forts at Pennal and Tomen y Mur. It was small, more like a police station.

Walk 18
Afon Melau

Exploring the basin where the Afon Melau drains down into the lowlands, this walk is an easy-to-follow track that takes you into some wild country. Starting from the village of Rhydymain, it crosses the Melau before heading up onto the slopes of the extinct volcano of Rhobell Fawr. The views out over the Aran range and the valley of the Afon Wnion are impressive, and the trail then heads down through forest on a return to the lowlands. It is probably the easiest way to experience a remote Welsh cwm.

The path leads through fields with Cadair Idris visible on the horizon

Start/finish	The bridge in Rhydymain over the Afon Eiddon /// movies.widget. brew (for car park)
Distance	11km (6¾ miles)
Ascent	340m
Time	3hr 15min
Terrain	Hill tracks and some tarmac
Maps	OS Explorer Map OL23 Cadair Idris & Llyn Tegid
Access	Rhydymain is a village on the A494 east of Dolgellau. There is a parking area in the east of the village near the village hall, or street parking. The village is at LL40 2AS.
Facilities	Nearest are in Dolgellau.

On the bridge over the **Afon Eiddon** in the village of **Rhydymain**, face upstream and take the road on the left-hand side, going up along the river. Pass the chapel and follow the tarmac as it bends left, up a ramp.

Go through the gate at the top and at the fork straight after, head right, uphill. As the track leaves the woods, head through the gate to continue on the trail, which runs between two walls, with fields on both sides.

After 400m, at the road, turn right and follow it ahead, downhill to the bridge Pont ar Felau, over the **Afon Melau**. Cross the bridge and go left straight after. After 100m, at the track fork with the gate on the left, take the right, stonier, option, uphill. The track soon narrows and enters a field.

Continue ahead on the sunken path with the fence on the left. Once through the next gate, continue

The Afon Eiddon heads through Rhydymain

ahead along the wall. The view here extends all the way to Cadair Idris, the bulk of mountain on the horizon, nearly 900m high.

On reaching the road, turn left. After 100m, go through the gate and turn right onto the footpath to follow the fence up. At the tarmac track, turn left and after 50m, turn right on the road. Head up, and at the fork after the gate, take the right-hand option, uphill. This is the track that leads up onto the hillside. It starts as tarmac and leads to an old quarry, around 1.5km further on. After the quarry the track becomes stony and heads through a forest at Ffridd y Castell.

RHOBELL FAWR

The mountain of Rhobell Fawr, whose cliffs and crags this walk gets you really close to, is an extinct volcano. Around 480 million years ago in the Ordovician period, the closure of the Iapetus Ocean (which was roughly where the modern Atlantic is) caused the subduction of the oceanic plate under Wales. This caused intense volcanic activity, and Rhobell Fawr was the first such area to become volcanically active.

Most of the mass of the mountain, and indeed the impressive crags passed at the highest point of this walk, is made from basalt, formed from the lava produced by this volcano. Rhobell Fawr is therefore very different to the rest of the Rhinogydd, which it is sometimes associated with, which are predominantly older sedimentary rock. It is volcanic rock from the Ordovician period that predominantly makes up the rocks of mountains such as Snowdon and Cadair Idris.

The trail heads up towards the flanks of the extinct volcano Rhobell Fawr

Looking across the Wnion valley towards the Arans

Leaving the forest, continue ahead past a set of gates, staying on the track, and cross a stream which is the infant Afon Melau. The track becomes rougher but is still easy to follow, past the crags of **Rhobell Fawr** at Graig Fâch. The view here encompasses the southern slopes of Rhobell Fawr and over to the Aran range, with wild and remote mountain scenery all around.

Eventually the track runs above a forest; head through the gate soon reached and arrive at a T-junction. Turn right and go straight ahead on the track downhill, with the slopes of Moel Cae'r-defaid on the left.

At the fork after 500m, take the left option, continuing ahead. This tarmac track becomes the road; continue along it for around 2.5km, through Ffridd yr Hengwrt and passing Braich-y-fedw, until arriving at a road junction. Turn left, and then after 200m, turn left onto a track. This is the track from the beginning of the walk, so follow it through the woods and back down to Rhydymain.

Walk 19
Llyn Arenig Fawr

A jewel on the side of the great Arenig Fawr, this walk leads across Afon Tryweryn, through the big-sky country near Llyn Celyn up to the mountain lake of Llyn Arenig Fawr. Visiting a bothy just next to the lake, and passing mountain crags, it then heads through the moorland valley of the Nant Aberderfel and drops down to the old railway line from Bala to Trawsfynydd, following it back through the valley.

A rest stop next to the dam of Llyn Arenig Fawr

Start/finish	Layby on the A4212 1.5km west of Llyn Celyn near Pantllwyni /// forms.trains.acids
Distance	10km (6 miles)
Ascent	130m
Time	2hr 45min
Terrain	Tracks, upland paths and old railway line. Nothing steep.
Maps	OS Explorer Map OL18 Harlech, Porthmadog & Bala/Y Bala
Access	Although there is a car park on the map on the western edge of Llyn Celyn at Cae-garnedd, there is no path from here to the walk. Instead, there is a layby on the main road 1.5km west of this car park. LL23 7PB leads roughly to the right area.
Facilities	Toilets at Cae-garnedd car park; café in outdoors centre to the east of Llyn Celyn.

From the layby on the A4212 west of **Llyn Celyn**, go to the road and turn right. Walk along the wide grassy verge for 400m and go through the gate on the right onto a track. Follow the track to cross the bridge over the **Afon Tryweryn**.

Beyond the bridge follow the rough path ahead, slightly left of centre, which follows some wooden posts. Soon, you'll pass a yellow arrow on a telegraph pole and head uphill onto a small hill. On reaching a clear path, turn right following the yellow arrows.

The path is level and heads across open ground around the slope of Foel Bodrenig. Pass to the right-hand side of a house that appears ahead, at Arenig. Cross the old (and now grassy) railway line to reach the road. Turn left on the road.

113

This **railway line**, which the walk returns along, is the old line from Bala to Trawsfynydd and Ffestiniog. Opened in 1882, it carried passengers and freight, including slate, until it ceased operating in the 1960s, at the same time that the road was built. The vast majority of the line is still accessible, aside from the section flooded during the creation of the Llyn Celyn reservoir.

After approximately 1km on the road, when the hillside of Moel y Garth is on the right and Llyn Celyn is visible below on the left, turn right to go through a gate with a 'Farmland' warning sign about keeping dogs on leads. Follow the track ahead uphill.

COFIWCH DRYWERYN

A sign near Bala to commemorate the flooding of Capel Celyn

Llyn Celyn is a reservoir, created in the early 1960s to provide water to Liverpool and the Wirral. At the time, its creation caused a huge amount of controversy, which still exists today. To create the reservoir, the Liverpool Corporation realised they would never get through Welsh planning permission and so took the issue straight to parliament in the form of the Tryweryn Reservoir Bill. Despite none of the 36 Welsh MPs voting for it, the bill passed, and construction of the dam began.

The flooding of the valley drowned the Welsh-speaking village of Capel Celyn, including 12 houses and farms, the chapel, school and post office. The residents protested through the streets of Liverpool to no avail. The dam opening ceremony lasted only a few minutes when chanting drowned out the speeches and the microphone cables were cut. Later, a pylon and a transformer were blown up.

The event became a galvanising force for Welsh nationalism and a driver for devolution. The words *Cofiwch Dryweryn* ('remember Tryweryn') were painted on a wall in Llanrhystud near Aberystwyth in the 1960s. Despite

Looking out over Llyn Celyn from the ascent alongside Arenig Fawr

being vandalised several times, most recently in 2019, it continues to be repaired, and there are now lots of similar signs around Wales, including on the roads around Bala.

This track leads over the low hillside for just over 2km, with the crags of Arenig Fawr ('great high ground') growing in stature ahead on the right. **Llyn Arenig Fawr** comes into view, and the track reaches the dam and a bench next to the water.

After admiring the lake, head down to a little hut. The hut is actually a bothy, so open to use for spending the night or just escaping the rain for something to eat. Pass the hut and follow the path onwards, without crossing the fence on the right. The path is small but clear, and leads down over moorland. Cross the stile just before the stream and head right to cross the footbridge over the **Nant Aberderfel**.

Beyond the footbridge continue straight ahead on the path, which soon bends left across the slope. It can be marshy but follow it on to reach a steeper part of the slope, a few metres high. Follow the path up this, and at a faint path junction, turn left onto a distinct grassy path to cross **Fridd y Fawnog**.

Follow this path for around 400m to reach a stone wall and a gate. Do not go through the gate but turn right and follow the wall, turning left when it does and following the path alongside it, passing Banc yr Arian.

On reaching the road, go straight across it and go ahead on the grassy track, which soon becomes a path. It swings right alongside a wall, and when the wall turns left, follow the path left also. Ignore side paths and leave the most obvious trail to head down to the bottom left wall corner of this open area. Cross the stile there and follow the path ahead, which soon bends right and runs down between two ruined walls towards Gwern-y-genau. The return section along the old railway line is on private land and is a permissive footpath. If there are signs indicating that it's closed, return along the road.

Continue ahead until passing through a gate and heading down to a track. Turn left and follow this track, which is the old railway. After 400m it swings up to the road. Turn right on the road, and 100m after crossing a bridge over the **Nant Aberderfel**, turn right again through a gate to follow a track a short distance to re-join the old railway line. Have a look out for the old railway bridge crossing the Nant Aberderfel, which has a large chunk of wall missing and is fenced off from the public.

Continue ahead on the level track, reaching the houses at Pant-yr-Hedydd. At the gate in front of the first house, bear right onto a rough path and follow the fence on the left along the hillside. After a few hundred metres, after passing a ruin and a pylon, the houses at Arenig appear again. When opposite them turn right to pick up the faint path from the start of the walk. Follow it around the hillside, down across the bridge and then up to the road. Turn left on the road to return to the layby.

Following the old railway embankment

Walk 20
Afon Lliw

The Afon Lliw is a short river, rushing down from the hills around Arenig Fawr to join Llyn Tegid in the valley. This walk explores the valley of the Lliw, a remote and infrequently visited place. The outward journey leads up onto moorland tracks and over rough ground, where the land sweeps away feeling more like an Asian steppe than a Welsh valley. Descending to the riverside itself, the walk then returns through farmland, with a highly recommended visit to the ruin of the 13th-century Castell Carndochan towards the end.

Looking through Pennant Lliw to Moel Llyfnant (Walk 20)

Start/finish	The bridge over the Afon Lliw in Dolhendre Isaf /// acting.otherwise. blocks
Distance	12km (7½ miles)
Ascent	340m
Time	3hr 45min
Terrain	Upland tracks and paths, with some road
Maps	OS Explorer Map OL23 Cadair Idris & Llyn Tegid
Access	Head out of Llanuwchllyn towards Bala, and shortly after crossing the bridge turn left onto the road signed to Trawsfynydd. Follow this road for 1 ½ miles to the bridge and phone box, where you can park. The postcode LL23 7TB leads down the right road.
Facilities	Pub in Llanuwchllyn. Further facilities in Bala.

From the bridge over the Afon Lliw in Dolhendre Isaf, beside the phone box, head up the road signposted to Trawsfynydd. Pass Dolhendre caravan park, then the old chapel and the entrance to the forest of **Coed Wenallt**. After just over 1km, turn right onto a side road with a dead-end sign, and a large boulder on the other side. Head through the farm at **Ty'n-y-bwlch** and continue along the track until it ends at the farm at **Trawscoed**. Turn left before the farm gate to go uphill on the track.

The track leads into moorland alongside Moel Hafod-yr-ŵyn, and then passes forestry as it heads into **Ffridd Trawsgoed**. At the end of the forest a large turning circle is reached with a hole on the right-hand side. Go straight ahead

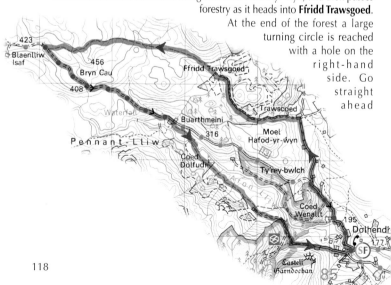

Crossing the Afon Erwent on the moorland traverse

through the gate. The peak ahead is Moel Llyfnant, which dominates the head of the valley and will be a constant companion for the rest of the walk.

Beyond this point the track becomes a path and at times is very indistinct. In general it leads straight on, and it often a wet hollow (in this case stay on the drier sides) so just follow your nose. In bad visibility it would be quite an ordeal.

Start by going ahead and following the path up to pass a 441m high knoll. Then the path goes downhill towards a series of streams including the **Afon Erwent**, around 1km after the gate. Ford or jump across these streams, the largest of which is 1m wide. After the last stream head up to the fence visible ahead, over very rough ground.

Follow the fence right to a gate, go through it and continue ahead up the rough path. Cross a knoll at **Bryn Cau** and continue downhill on an extremely indistinct path. In general, go ahead up the small marshy valley after the knoll. Towards the end of the valley the rough path reappears and heads over the rise on the left. Or just head left anytime.

From the rise, a farm at **Blaenlliw Isaf** comes into view, with a forest on top of the hill opposite. Follow the path down to the road and turn left into **Pennant Lliw**.

Follow the road for 2km to **Buarthmeini**. Cross the bridge over the Afon Erwent just before the farm. Pass the farm, cross a stream and then turn right through a gate onto a bridleway. Look back up the Afon Lliw that runs through the valley to see the waterfall.

Follow the vague path, which bends left and runs to the left of a ruined stone wall. Go through a gate and continue ahead with a fence on the right. After 100m cross a footbridge over the river and then turn immediately left to follow the river. As the river bends left, follow a small tributary stream right a short distance to cross a concrete bridge.

Head up the grassy path, which winds on, and soon goes through a gate in a fence. Continue in the same direction, heading down through a meadow and crossing a wooden footbridge. The woodland of **Coed Dolfudr** is up on the right.

The path becomes quite obscure. In general, head in the direction of the large pole on the small hill ahead. On reaching a fence, do not go through it but turn right, uphill to reach the fence corner. Follow the top of the fence towards the farm at Craig-y-tân and go through a gate leading towards the farm. Cross the field to another gate visible 100m away, going through this onto a stony track.

Turn right on the track and follow it directly past the left-hand side of the farm and onwards, downhill through a forest.

Optional extension to Castell Carndochan (30min)

An optional out-and-back route leads up to the ruins of Castell Carndochan, on the hill on the right. After the forest, cross the stream and take the gate on the

The ruins of Castell Carndochan high above the valley

right. Follow the track, which zig-zags up, and as it levels a junction is reached. Turn left here and follow the rough path over the hillside towards the ruin, which is visible ahead. Explore the castle, with its extensive views over the valley and the mountains around Aran Fawddwy. Return the same way back to the track.

Castell Carndochan itself is mostly rubble but you can clearly see the outline of parts of the four towers and the walls. Occupying a key defensive position above the valley, it was thought to have been built by Llywelyn the Great in the 13th century and perhaps destroyed by the English on their invasion at the end of the 13th century.

To continue the main walk, carry on along the track, which then becomes a road and reaches a junction at Ty-du. Turn left to arrive back at the bridge and the phone box.

Walk 21

Gwastadros

This short walk takes you up a wonderful small hill on the outskirts of Bala. These smaller hills are too often overlooked, and though the way to it is somewhat confusing, it is worth the effort, especially for the views. Starting from the banks of Llyn Tegid, the trail leads up through woodland onto the flanks of Moel y Garnedd, where myriad paths can be used to explore the summit area and surrounding clusters of trees before returning the same way. The whole summit area is on open access land, so wander where you wish.

Looking down towards Llyn Tegid from the slopes of Moel y Garnedd

Start/finish	Mary Jones World car park /// primary.other.windmills
Distance	6km (3¾ miles)
Ascent	200m
Time	2hr
Terrain	Hill paths
Maps	OS Explorer Map OL18 Harlech, Porthmadog & Bala/Y Bala
Access	Mary Jones World lies on the A494 a short drive from Bala on the banks of the lake. As well as the cark park there, there is another car park not far from the entrance owned by the National Park. Postcode is LL23 7YF.
Facilities	Café at Mary Jones World. Further facilities in Bala.

Mary Jones World is a heritage centre dedicated to the story of Mary Jones, who in 1800 walked 26 miles barefoot to Bala to buy a bible, after having saved money for it for 5 years. Centre open April to October. www.bydmaryjonesworld.org.uk

From the car park in Byd Mary Jones World at **Llanycil**, on the shore of **Llyn Tegid**, head back to the main road and turn left. After 50m turn right and cross the road to reach the entrance of **Fronfeuno Farm**. Walk up the middle of the three tracks.

As the track bends right after 200m, go ahead onto a footpath that skirts to the left-hand side of a woodland. Soon, head through a small gate to enter woodland and continue along the path through the trees, for around 300m.

Leave the woods at the far end into a field. Follow the path ahead through the field, which is indistinct. Towards the top end, head towards the left-hand side of the field and cross the footbridge over the Aber Gwenwyn-feirch.

Beyond the footbridge head through the gate and go uphill across the field to pass through another gate. Cross the field beyond and pass through the gate to follow a track between buildings to a tarmac track at Plas Moel-y-Garnedd (oddly

123

The woodland surrounding Fronfeuno Farm and Aber Gwenwyn-feirch

just marked as **Moel-y-garnedd** on the OS 1:50,000 map). Turn right towards the caravan park, uphill.

At the fork at the site entrance, take the right option and follow it as it bends left, uphill. In-between caravans 23 and 24, go through a gate into a field. Head straight across this field (slightly right) to find a gate with a yellow footpath arrow. Once through this gate you are on the open hillside of **Gwastadros**. The little hut at Ty-newydd is visible over on the left.

The best way to reach the summit from here is to cross the stream soon after the gate. There are many braided paths leading onwards, so follow your nose and head up towards the left-hand side of the highest trees visible on the hill, on the horizon. There are frequent places to admire the view back down over Bala Lake/Llyn Tegid, the largest natural lake in Wales, at nearly 5km² and 42m deep.

Once at the left-hand side of these trees, it is clear that the ones nearest are in a circular enclosure. Shortly after this enclosure, heading up, there is a path fork. Take the left-hand option, heading for the high point of the hill. There is a rocky outcrop, and a marsh here, which can be bypassed by going a bit to the right.

The high point is marked by a trig point, the summit of Moel y Garnedd at 360m, with an astonishing view that ranges from Llyn Tegid and the hills east of Snowdonia, all the way to the Arenigs and the Arans.

Return the same way you have come. If the paths on the way down are confusing, use the clearly visible caravan park to navigate by.

Walk 22
Bala Lake/Llyn Tegid

*Bala Lake is the largest natural lake in Wales, a beautiful spot rich in
aquatic life and popular for watersports. Unfortunately it has roads right
next to it on both sides, so walking along the shore is difficult. This route is the
best way to see it, wandering along the hillsides and farms above
the lake, with a fantastic view of it for the whole length, then dropping
down to touch the shore again at the end. As it starts from
Llangower on the south shore, it is possible to take the lakeside
railway out from Bala and then walk back. Alongside views of the
lake you'll see beautiful woodlands, and gaze over
to the hills on the horizon.*

Llyn Tegid from Bala, with the Arans rising up on the horizon

Start	Car park in Llangower station /// land.costs.dreamers
Finish	The Loch Café, Y Bala /// worlds.pool.social
Distance	7.5km (4¾ miles)
Ascent	250m
Time	2hr 30min
Terrain	Farmland and woodland paths
Maps	OS Explorer Map OL23 Cadair Idris & Llyn Tegid; OS Explorer Map OL18 Harlech, Porthmadog & Bala/Y Bala
Access	Llangower is on the B4403 south of Bala Lake. The station car park is off the main road at LL23 7BY. The postcode for the lakeside car park and Loch Café in Bala is LL23 7SR.
Facilities	Toilets at Llangower. Pubs, shops and cafés in Bala.
Note	If you wish to get the train out and walk back, see www.bala-lake-railway.co.uk for the timetable.

There is a picnic area at the car park, and it is possible to reach the lakeshore by crossing the railway. From the Bala Lake Railway station car park in Llangower, head out onto the road and turn left. Take the first road on the right, opposite the graveyard. At the immediate fork, keep right. After 400m the road crosses a stream. Immediately afterwards turn left off the road through a gate onto a foot-path uphill, following the stream.

LLYN TEGID (BALA LAKE)

Llyn Tegid ('fair lake') or as it's often called in English, Bala Lake, is Wales' largest natural lake, though it too now has its height controlled by a weir. Its long length and straight parallel sides are characteristic of a glacial rib-bon lake. The glacier would have gouged out the hollow, encouraged by the whole valley sitting on a more easily weathered geological fault. The ter-minal moraine of the glacier is the raised land where Y Bala town now sits.

The lake is famous as the last stronghold of the gwyniad, a fish found only here and in Llyn Arenig Fawr, where several were released as an insur-ance policy as the main population in Llyn Tegid is under threat from the invasive ruffe.

There is a legend that under the lake lies the town of Old Bala. The town was flooded when the cover on a spring was left open, or opened by the devil, and the waters rushed out and covered the town. The current town of Bala is said to be awaiting the same fate.

After 150m, cross the footbridge on the left when it appears, and head up the other side. In the field follow the faint path across, indicated by the yellow-topped post. At the far end of the field go through a gate and bear left. Head down to the right-hand side of the buildings at Ty-cerig, passing a barn. Turn right along the track.

The track becomes a path into **Glyn Gower**. Follow it to a junction with a substantial track. Turn left, cross the bridge over **Nant Rhydwen** and head up the other side to meet the road; turn left to follow the road under Coed yr Allt. After 300m turn right onto a track, pass a farm, and 100m later at a junction with a footpath post, turn right, uphill. Follow this path past the right-hand side of the house, Pant-yr-onen. When you reach a track, follow it ahead through a gate. Shortly after take a path on the left along the fence.

Continue ahead through the pretty woods of Coed Pant-yr-onen and Coed y Gilwern along the fence. At the edge of the woods a footpath sign sends you downhill on the left. Follow a small stream, and shortly after the next gate turn right to cross the stream at a footpath post. Head diagonally downhill through the next field, passing big oaks and crossing a footbridge.

127

Crossing the Nant Rhyd-wen just above Llangower

The trail through Bryniau Golau looking down on Llyn Tegid

In the next field continue ahead keeping the fence on the left. Shortly after crossing a small stream the distinct path heads uphill away from the fence. It crosses another stream and continues up, over the open fields at **Bryniau Golau**, with excellent views of **Bala Lake/Llyn Tegid** on the left. Bala itself first comes into view from the climb up this slope. It is closer than it looks!

On reaching a fence with a gate and a metal footpath post, go through the gate and turn left on the track downhill. Reach the road and turn left, then turn right onto a path after around 20m. Follow the grassy path, which heads towards **Y Bala** and follows a drainage ditch/stream. Ignore faint paths leading off to the left.

The path descends in a zig-zag to a gate. Go through it and follow the path ahead, crossing a stream at Ffrîdd Goed and heading up the other bank. Shortly follow the fence on the left, which descends. Continue for 500m to arrive at a tarmac track and a golf course. Turn right and head along the tarmac that leads through the middle of the buildings, behind the club house and **Bala Lakeside Hotel**.

Go ahead through the car park at the back onto a track. Pass another house, and then 200m further on go left through a gate into a field, where there is a footpath sign. Cross the field with the fence on the left, cross a gate/stile and head diagonally across the field beyond. Pass through a gate to cross a footbridge over the Bala Lake Railway to Bala Station and follow the path ahead to the road.

The **earthworks** on the right-hand side as you leave the station are the site of a motte and bailey, built by the Normans as far back as the 11th century. There would have been a fortified wooden enclosure on top. This site was important in guarding where the River Dee leaves Llyn Tegid.

Cross the road and go straight ahead over the old bridge. Continue ahead along pavement over new bridge **Pont Mwnwgl-y-llyn** over the River Dee/Afon Dyfrdwy and follow the pavement at the next road junction to stay next to the lake. At the entrance to the 30 zone turn left onto a path to stay next to the lake. Follow this path all the way to the lakeside parking and The Loch Café. From here it is also possible to turn right on the road to make your way to Y Bala town centre.

CADAIR IDRIS
TO THE DYFI

The Dolgoch Falls on the Nant Dol-goch tumbles down rocks into the valley (Walk 27)

Walk 23
Cwm Cywarch

*Cwm Cywarch lies in the Aran mountains, totally hidden from the cars
rushing past on the main road north. From Dinas Mawddwy, with its Alpine
setting, the walk heads gradually round the side of Foel Benddin
into the Cwm, the view growing ever more magnificent with the
crags of Craig Cywarch rising up ahead. Surrounded by high peaks, the
circuit of the valley concludes with a wander along the banks of the
Afon Dyfi back to Dinas Mawddwy.*

Looking out over Cwm Cywarch and up to Craig Cywarch with
streams tumbling off the plateau

Start/finish	The road junction in Dinas Mawddwy outside the Red Lion/Y Llew Coch /// bribing.piglets.chitchat
Distance	11km (6½ miles)
Ascent	160m
Time	3hr
Terrain	Tarmac track and road, with some field paths
Maps	OS Explorer Map OL23 Cadair Idris & Llyn Tegid
Access	Dinas Mawddwy lies just off the A470 in-between Dolgellau and Machynlleth. The car park is just off the cross-roads next to the Red Lion pub. Postcode for the Red Lion is SY20 9JA.posted off the A493 just east of Fairbourne. Postcode is LL39 1BQ.
Facilities	Pub, café and post office shop in Dinas Mawddwy.

From the road junction in **Dinas Mawddwy** outside the Red Lion, follow the road downhill towards Bala, with the pub on the right. After 300m, cross the stream at Pont Dôl-y-bont and turn immediately left onto a track at the **caravan park entrance**, then right up a sloping path.

The village of **Dinas Mawddwy** is an old settlement, with Iron Age forts nearby and a thriving community complete with stories of local bandits in the Middle Ages. In the 19th century it joined the slate revolution, and the main quarry is hidden on the side of Foel Dinas, behind the village. Just to the south, the former railway terminus, built to move slate south to Machynlleth, has been converted into the woollen mill and craft centre Meirion Mill (**www.meirionmill.co.uk**).

Go through a gate after 50m and continue ahead up the path. At the path

133

fork after the caravans, go left, downhill, than at another fork after 30m, go right, uphill. The path heads up to an old track running under a forest. Turn right onto this track.

After 600m, the track reaches a road junction. Go left on the road, uphill. The road leads into the valley of **Cwm Cywarch** and is mostly flat. Follow it for 2km, pass through Deunant-mawr Farm and continue ahead when the road becomes a track. At the head of the valley rises Craig Cywarch, the impressive crags of Glasgwm, with various streams falling off the plateau above.

Pass the ruins at Nant yr Henfaes and continue ahead on what is now a dirt track. The track drops down to follow the **Afon Cywarch** and arrives at a road with a bridge on the right; turn left here. The road soon leads across an open meadow at **Fawnog Fawr**; head straight across it and exit the other end on the road towards the car park.

200m after the end of the meadow, cross the footbridge on the right, next to the ford. At the fork just after the bridge, take the left-hand option. This path heads up through a yard and up a sunken path, and soon swings right between fences. Shortly after this, the path swings left, uphill, with a footpath arrow and a metal sign. At this point, do not follow the path uphill but instead go through the gate/ stile ahead into the field. Continue straight ahead, keeping the fence on the right and staying at the same height.

Pass the ruin at Ty'n-y-ddol and cross over the fence on the right via a stile next to two metal gates. Continue ahead in the same direction as before with

Following the road into Cwm Cywarch

the fence now on the left. Pass through two fields and join a track at **Ty'n-y-twll**. Follow the track straight past the front of the house and up to two gates. Go through the right-hand gate and continue ahead through two fields and then pass through a wooded streamside on a dirt track.

Go straight across the field on the other side onto a track through woods, then turn left off the track into a field, to stay in the same direction. Head across the field, slightly uphill, to reach a stile and footpath arrow just in front of a ruined stone house near **Ty'n-y-maes**. Cross the stile to pass to the right of the house. Cross a stile/gate and continue over a field to join a track next to a barn.

Continue ahead on the track down to the road. Turn left and follow the road for 2km, past **Bryn Sion**, to the road junction near **Aber Cywarch**. Turn left on the road, and after 50m, turn right onto a path to cross the footbridge over the Afon Dyfi. Beyond the bridge, turn right to follow the river.

This is the young **Afon Dyfi**, which heads south to flow through Machynlleth and then heads west to the Irish Sea, forming the heart of the protected area of the Dyfi Biosphere Reserve.

Beyond the first field, cross a stile into a wood and continue along the river. The path leads through another field, through a gate, and then begins rising up

Dinas Mawddwy, on the banks of the Afon Dyfi

The Afon Dyfi makes its way through woodland on route to Dinas Mawddwy

the slope away from the river. Soon Dinas Mawddwy appears ahead and the path levels; when the path enters an open field and becomes faint, continue straight ahead towards a house.

At the corner of a field, which looks like an old orchard, the path leads to a gate. Go through it and follow the path ahead past an old concrete wall corner. Go through the next gate on the right after this corner. Head across the field to the left-hand corner of the building.

Go through the gate to reach a farmyard, cross it and exit on the left-hand side onto a track. After 50m at a fork, go through a gate on the right and follow the track ahead. This reaches the Afon Dyfi; follow it to cross a footbridge and go ahead along the track to the road. Turn left on the road to return to Dinas Mawddwy.

Walk 24
Castell y Bere

This wild and remote head of the Dysynni Valley is brooded over by the great Cadair Idris, and surrounded by its foothills. Starting at the site of Llywelyn the Great's fortress of Castell y Bere, the walk takes you on a circuit of this part of the valley, hugging the base of the hills and visiting the site of Mary Jones' House. Crossing the valley and the river, it gives you a great appreciation of the castle's presence in the valley and views up to the surrounding peaks. An easy walk following paths and the odd bit of road, it is amazing to think that in the 13th century there were plans for an English town to be created here.

Castell y Bere held a key defensive position in Dryffryn Dysynni

Start/finish	Castell y Bere car park /// flat.chosen.rehearsed
Distance	7km (4½ miles)
Ascent	120m
Time	2hr
Terrain	Farmland paths and some road
Maps	OS Explorer Map OL23 Cadair Idris & Llyn Tegid
Access	Castell y Bere is signposted on the road north out of Abergynolwyn. There is a small car park next to the castle entrance, and another one down in Llanfihangel-y-pennant. The rough postcode is LL36 9TP.
Facilities	None. Café and pub in Abergynolwyn.

Use the gate behind the **car park** to explore the site of **Castell y Bere**, which from here looks like a small wooded hill. Afterwards, return to the car park and, facing the road, turn left and walk along it. There is a sign to Ty'n y Ddôl.

Castell y Bere is a true Welsh castle, built by Llywelyn the Great to defend the southern borders of Gwynedd and protect his cattle lands. Construction began in 1221 using the key defence of the rocky hill in the middle of the valley. The defences, particularly around the gatehouse, were state of the art, and include two gate towers, a drawbridge and a portcullis. The ditch under the drawbridge is easy to see at the entrance, and would have proved a formidable defence. The castle was taken by Edward I in 1283, and he hoped to establish an English town here, a project that came to naught.

Head through **Llanfihangel-y-pennant** and pass **Mary Jones' Chapel**, actually St Michael's Church, and at the road fork straight afterwards, continue

138

Looking up the valley of the Afon Cadair towards the foothills of Cadair Idris

ahead (the right-hand option). There has been a church on this site since the 13th century, and the font is believed to be from the castle.

After 500m further on the road, turn right off the road onto a footpath going uphill and leading to the right side of the farm at **Tynyfach**. At the track fork after the gate, go right, uphill. The track rises then levels off.

Continue along this track over a stream until a gate/stile appears on the left. Cross the stile and go downhill through the field, aiming for the bridge. The best way to reach the bridge is to follow the wall down, go through a gap on the right, continue following it down to the bottom until you can go left through a gate and continue a short way to the bridge.

After crossing the footbridge over the **Afon Cadair**, go up the field on the other side through a gate. Turn left on the track and follow it down past the house at **Gwastadfryn**. Continue on this track to pass Mary Jones' House at **Ty'n-y-Ddôl**.

Mary Jones has left a large legacy because of a single act she made, which was built up over many years. At the age of 10 she decided that she wanted her own bible, which cost a huge amount at the time. She saved for five years and in 1800, aged 15, walked the 26 miles barefoot from this house to Bala to buy one from Rev. Thomas Charles. As all the bibles he had were promised to others, he is said to have given her his own as he was so moved by her story. He went on to help establish the Bible Society, which distributes bibles around the world.

Mary Jones' Chapel in Llanfihangel-y-pennant

Immediately after the house, at the junction, go straight ahead onto the footpath, staying on the right side of the Afon Cadair. After 300m at the house at Gernos, go through the gate and follow the path past the house on the left. Continue along the path ahead.

The path passes the bridge to a farm and continues on through the next field to a wall. Follow the wall right and then ahead again, along the line of the telegraph poles, through a gate with a white arrow.

Continue ahead following this wall for around 800m, crossing a few intersecting walls. It slowly bends to the right following the hillside and passes to the right of the farm at Pen-y-meini. Once next to the farm, cross the stile with the yellow-topped post and cross the stream. Head left a short distance through a gate onto the road.

Turn left on the road and follow it for just over 1km to a junction. At the junction, turn left and follow the road round to the right, past the **post box**, towards the farm at **Caerberllan**. Continue past the farm gates and go through the next gate on the left, 100m further on.

Follow the track up into a field, where it disappears. Continue straight ahead across the field and through scattered trees, keeping at the same height. A faint path is sometimes visible, and there is a fence on the left.

Once across the field, there is a grassy track and a set of two gates in parallel fences. Go through both gates and continue ahead on the track. Keep going along the track until opposite Castell y Bere, which soon appears ahead on its prominent outcrop. Look out for an old green rusted kissing gate on the left. Go through this gate and follow the path diagonally ahead through the field.

The car park is soon visible ahead, and the path reaches the road. Cross the stile and turn right on the road to return to the car park.

Walk 25
Abergynolwyn

*Standing at the confluence of the Afon Dysynni and the Nant Gwernol,
Abergynolwyn is a peaceful former slate village surrounded by striking slopes
and forest. This walk leads up past the Talyllyn railway into the forest around
Foel Fawr and heads into the valley of the Nant Gwernol, with views up to the
Tarren hills and the foothills of Cadair Idris. It includes an exploration of the
disused Bryn Eglwys slate quarry before following a beautiful streamside path
back into the village.*

Looking down on Abergynolwyn and the surrounding hills

Start/finish	Car park in Abergynolwyn beside the community centre ///skid. blank.cities
Distance	8.3km (5¼ miles)
Ascent	290m
Time	2hr 45min
Terrain	Forest tracks
Maps	OS Explorer Map OL23 Cadair Idris & Llyn Tegid
Access	Abergynolwyn lies just up the B4405 from Twywn. The postcode for the car park (free) is LL36 9UU.
Facilities	Abergynolwyn has a pub and a café. The closest shops are in Twywn.

From the car park in **Abergynolwyn**, go to the **B4405** main road and turn left. Follow the road past the Railway Inn, towards Abergynolwyn Station. Once past the last house on the left, at **Hendre**, turn left down a track. There is a footpath sign, and the track is just before the national speed limit sign on the road.

The track bends right. Follow it up and over the railway line. At the T-junction after the railway, at the Nant Gwernol Forest sign, turn right. The track slowly rises, and after 300m, bends left.

Follow it up, where there are excellent views down over Abergynolwyn and up to Cadair Idris. The track turns right to enter the valley along the slopes of **Foel Fawr**. At the track fork, go left. The track bends left and passes the Nant Moelfre. After descending for 500m past the stream, go right at the fork.

After another 500m, turn right onto a footpath uphill, opposite a post with a blue/white footprint. The path leads up in a loop to view the remains of the **Bryn Eglwys quarry**. Eventually it descends to the track, at a turning circle.

Opening in the 1840s, the **Bryn Eglwys quarry** extracted slate from the same veins that run east to Corris. It was due to the difficulty in getting the slate over the mountain to Aberdyfi that the Talyllyn railway was built, enabling the slate to quickly

The Nant Gwernol, making its way through the woodland of Abergynolwyn

The remains of the Bryn Eglwys slate quarry

reach the sea. At its height, the quarry employed more than 300 men, and despite several closures, continued operating in some form until a serious collapse in 1949, so lasting for just over 100 years and producing around 300,000 tons of slate. Now the slopes around the quarry are used for plantation forestry, and the railway has a new life as a tourist attraction. This isn't a total change in purpose, as the original railway was built to carry people as well as slate.

Turn right to follow the path; at a fork past a yellow-topped post, take the left-hand option to continue ahead. After 100m it bends left. Follow it through woodland past mine tips and shafts. When it reaches a crossroads of tracks, continue straight on, then after 200m turn left at the signpost to the station.

Go through a kissing gate onto a path downhill into the woodland of Coed Hendrewallog and Coed Nant Gwernol. At the fork halfway down, turn left down the stony path. There are many enticing pools for bathing along the stream, so if it's a hot day bring something to take a dip in!

Follow the path down to the **Nant Gwernol** and along it. Do not cross the first bridge, and keep on the right of the stream. Later on, when the path forks just above the bridge to the **Nant Gwernol Station**, take the left fork but do not cross the bridge, keeping to the path on the right of the stream. When this joins a minor road, turn left to descend to Abergynolwyn and you'll soon arrive at the village centre and car park.

Walk 26
Birds' Rock

The low saddles that separate the valleys of the Afon Dysynni and the Afon Fathew allow a circular walk that does not gain a huge amount in height but allows the exploration of two beautiful valleys. Leading away from Dolgoch past Abertrinant, the route drops down through woodland to Dyffryn Dysynni and wanders past the inspiring bulk of Birds' Rock, definitely a sight and sound in breeding season. It then follows the river before branching off along tracks to return to the other side of the hills, finishing through the woods and fields of Tan-y-coed.

Following the road through Dyffryn Dysynni past Birds' Rock

Start/finish	Dolgoch café car park /// fabric.purse.handle
Distance	10.5km (6¾ miles)
Ascent	270m
Time	3hr 15min
Terrain	Field paths, with some tracks and road
Maps	OS Explorer Map OL23 Cadair Idris & Llyn Tegid
Access	Dolgoch lies on the B4405 inland from Tywyn. It is signposted off the road, and can be found at LL36 9UW.
Facilities	Café at Dolgoch. Pub further up the road at Abergynolwyn and further facilities in Tywyn.

From the car park in **Dolgoch**, go onto the road and turn left (straight ahead). After 200m, as the road bends left, go ahead onto the footpath and turn left. Most visitors to Dolgoch come to see the waterfalls (Walk 27), which are just a short walk from the same starting point.

Follow the path through the field. At the footpath sign on the far side, do not go through the gate but turn right, uphill. Continue ahead on this path, which soon levels off, following it through several fields. There are plenty of yellow arrows or yellow posts. On reaching a fence before a tarmac track, turn right up towards the farm at **Tŷ-mawr**. Go through the gate to reach the tarmac track and turn right up towards the farm.

When next to the farmhouse, turn left and head through the gate 20m away.

Go ahead through another gate, then bear left to go through a small gate with a white arrow and continue ahead with the hedge on the right. After 200m, when the hedge ends, continue

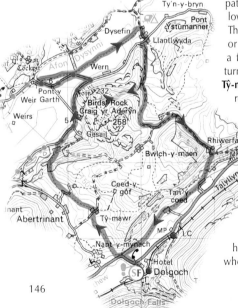

Following the path through fields near Abertrinant

ahead. Go through the small gate at the other side of the field. Beyond the gate, walk 50m further to reach an old concrete track. Go left on it to continue in the same direction as before. On reaching a ruin, go ahead on the grassy path.

Keeping the fence on the left leads ahead to a small gate into a field. Continue ahead across this field, aiming for a gap between the woodlands. Go through the gate on the right-hand side of this gap, which soon comes into view, into Coed y Tyno.

Follow the path downhill through the woods to the road running through Dyffryn Dysynni and turn right. Follow the road for around 1km, right under the crags of **Birds' Rock/Craig yr Aderyn**.

Birds' Rock is named after the large number of birds that breed there. Alongside other species including the barn owl and peregrine falcon, the site is protected for choughs, which although relatively common in Snowdonia are rare in the UK as a whole. It is also the largest inland breeding site in Wales for cormorants, a species which normally breeds on sea cliffs. The lower of the two summits is crowned with an Iron Age hill fort, and Roman remains have also been found up there. The higher summit has a Bronze Age cairn on top.

At the road junction, turn left and follow the road for around 600m to the bridge **Pont y Garth**. Just before it, turn right onto the footpath, which runs along the top of the embankment next to the **Afon Dysynni**. Follow the embankment 1.5km to the end, where there is a bench and a track into a stand of trees.

The **Afon Dysynni** is thought to have changed course during the last Ice Age, when a landslide blocked its former route west at Abergynolwyn, forcing it to move north and flow through this valley.

Join the track and follow it ahead. Just before the gate, take the path on the right of the fence to a tarmac track and turn right through the **campsite** at **Llanllwyda**.

At the road, turn right and after 150m turn left through the gate onto the path uphill. On meeting another stone path, continue ahead uphill. After roughly 500m, just before a gate, there is a path on the right up to Birds' Rock.

Optional detour to Birds' Rock (45min)

To reach the summit of Birds' Rock, follow this path up to the summit at 233m (which is not the main summit of this hill), also the site of an Iron Age fort. Return the same way and continue on the path through the gate.

Go through the gate ahead. The path is faint but continues rising up around the hill. Head up the next field, keeping the wall and stream on the left. Towards the top corner of the field, turn left through a gate and head along a level path across a field to another gate.

Once through the gate, continue on the path. At the tarmac track, go left and follow this for 300m above Gelli-ddraenen, then through a gate and into a forest. After 600m, when passing some buildings at **Rhiwerfa**, the road starts going downhill. Turn right soon after this onto a path leading steeply down through the trees.

Follow this path down to the farm at Tan-y-coed-uchaf. Pass the buildings and when the path turns left to join a concrete track, do not follow it but go ahead through a gate, to continue on a path running along the hillside at the same level. It follows the telegraph poles, with the fence on the left.

After 500m, on arriving at tarmac next to the house at Tan-y-coed-isaf, turn right and go through the gate with the yellow arrow. Continue following this path along, all the way to the road corner which appears on the left after Dolgoch car park also becomes visible. At the road corner, turn left off the path onto the road and go ahead along the road to return to the car park.

Dolgoch Falls

This short walk is an excellent outing to the waterfalls – which form as the Nant Dol-goch cascades down the steps in the gorge – and also to the surrounding woodland. Though reasonably steep, there is plenty of interest, from ferns clinging on to rock walls, to glimpses of the stream cutting into the rock. At the top there is a picnic spot with some good pools to paddle in, before the trail heads down the other side and returns to the café.

Dolgoch Falls, plunging through the woods from the Tarren range

Start/finish	Dolgoch car park /// fabric.purse.handle
Distance	2.6km (1¾ miles)
Ascent	120m
Time	1hr
Terrain	Woodland paths
Maps	OS Explorer Map OL23 Cadair Idris & Llyn Tegid
Access	Dolgoch lies on the B4405 inland from Tywyn. It is signposted off the road, and can be found at LL36 9UW.
Facilities	Café at Dolgoch. Pub further up the road at Abergynolwyn and further facilities in Tywyn.

From the **car park** at Dolgoch ('red meadow'), head to the stream and turn left to follow the path past the café. Head through the gate and continue straight on, next to the stream of the Nant Dol-goch. The viaduct holds the Talyllyn railway, which was built to transport slate from Bryn Eglwys quarry down to Tywyn. It is now purely used for transporting people.

Go under the viaduct and turn right to cross the **bridge** over the stream; follow the path on the other side, which passes the **Dolgoch Falls** and then zig-zags up. At the first path junction, go left to reach a viewing area and then return and continue up, ignoring a path with a no entry sign.

At a distinct path fork, take the option right, uphill. Ignore the path that crosses the stream ahead via a small wooden bridge and continue zig-zagging up. With views of the surrounding hills increasing, the path eventually crosses a stream via a stone slab. Continue onwards, traversing the slope.

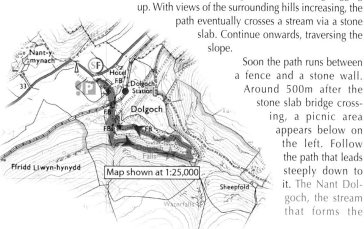

Soon the path runs between a fence and a stone wall. Around 500m after the stone slab bridge crossing, a picnic area appears below on the left. Follow the path that leads steeply down to it. The Nant Dolgoch, the stream that forms the

150

Dolgoch Falls, has its source up on the slopes of Tarrenhendre, the most southerly 2000ft mountain in Snowdonia.

Cross the footbridge and follow the path, which bends left on the other side. On reaching steps which go downhill on the left, head down them to reach the stream. Stay on the path on the right side of the river, seeing various small waterfalls and old mine entrances. The path eventually winds back down to beneath the main falls.

Stay next to the stream on the path back under the viaduct to return to the café and the car park.

One of the many footbridges over the Nant Dol-goch, allowing you to explore the woods

Walk 28
Cwm Ratgoed

This exploration of the banks of the Afon Dulas out of Corris is an excellent introduction to the valleys of south Snowdonia that once resounded with the sound of slate quarrying. Passing rolling forested hills, the trail passes Aberllefenni and completes a circuit of the secluded Cwm Ratgoed, with the hidden remains of Ratgoed Hall serving as a reminder of the industry that once was. Following easy tracks through forestry – the latest industry to take over the hillsides – it heads back out of the valley in view of the giant cavern of Twll Golau.

Entering Cwm Ratgoed near Cymerau farm

Start/finish	Corris car park /// devotion.machine.dunk
Distance	13.3km (8¼ miles)
Ascent	200m
Time	4hr
Terrain	Lowland tracks and some woodland paths
Maps	OS Explorer Map OL23 Cadair Idris & Llyn Tegid
Access	Corris is signposted just off the A487 north of Machynlleth. The car park is in the centre of the village next to the steam railway museum. The postcode is SY20 9SH.
Facilities	Pub and shop in Corris.

From the car park at the steam railway museum, head back to the main road through the village and turn right. Follow the road over the bridge, and take the next road on the right (Minffordd Street), at the crossroads. Follow this road for 300m down to cross a bridge over the **Afon Dulas** and then up the other side.

100m after the bridge, turn left onto a footpath where there is a wooden footpath post on the left of the road with a black metal rusted bench next to it. On the right is the entrance to Pentre Farm.

Follow this path, and when it leaves the trees, **Corris** is visible on the left. The path forks just after passing a steep drop (a disused quarry); take the left-hand fork, which goes downhill. The path now follows the Afon Dulas for 1km or so, where it joins a track next to some green huts at Caecenau.

Beyond the green hut cross the bridge and follow the track as it bends left. At the T-junction,

153

The path leads through Coed Maes-mawr near Aberllefenni

SNOWDONIAN SLATE MINING

Twll Golau, a great chamber high on the old slate mine above Aberllefenni

Aberllefenni and Corris form the heart of what was a vibrant slate mining industry in the southern part of Snowdonia, exploiting an accessible series of slate veins that run through the valley. Owing to the immense pressure applied to the rock by geological processes, slate is easy to split and forms clean faces and edges, a factor that was exploited for hundreds of years. It was in the second half of the 19th century though, with the ability to transport slate across the country and around the world, when the slate revolution kicked off in Wales.

Slates of the best quality could be cut so fine they could be used as roof tiles, a vital building material that made Welsh slate famous and drove the economy in the area. The industry eventually declined due to more competitive foreign imports and the sapping of the workforce who went to fight in the world wars. Aberllefenni slate quarry, with its giant hole of Twll Golau visible above the spoil tips, outlasted the rest in the area and only closed in 2003, though the nearby workshop is still in operation today.

turn right. Continue ahead on this track for 500m, through Coed Caecenau and Coed Maes-mawr, part of the Dolfriog Woods, on the slopes of **Moel Heulen**.

When the track bends left and goes downhill, take the path on the right, to continue in the same direction as before. There is a footpath arrow and a sign saying 'Foel Friog Footpath'. The path runs at the base of the wood, and the village of **Aberllefenni** is visible over fields on the left.

At the path fork straight after the ruin, continue ahead. Soon the view reaches down into a gorge on the left, where the **Nant Esgair-neiriau** runs. On reaching the footbridge, cross it and at the fork straight after, go left, uphill. Follow the yellow footpath arrows on an undulating path ahead. After 100m, at the path fork, when the path swings left and another path continues ahead, and there are two footpath posts; follow the path left, downhill.

Cross the footbridge and follow the path ahead to the road; on the road turn right and walk along it. As the road bends left past a house, ignore the track on the left and continue along the road for 300m. As it bends right and crosses the stream, take the next track on the left, with a footpath post to **Cymerau Farm**. Follow the track uphill towards the farm and then as it bends left to pass the farm. 100m after the farm, take the next track on the right, uphill, through a gate, then almost immediately left onto a path, doubling back on yourself, to walk on the right-hand side of a stone wall.

The path bends right after 50m to enter **Cwm Ratgoed**; continue above the fence/wall ahead. There is an awkward gate, which may need to be untied or climbed over. Traverse the fields ahead, and on arriving above a slate spoil tip, join a path that heads diagonally down it, to join the track below.

A ruined slate mine building in Cwm Ratgoed

On the track turn right and follow it ahead into the back end of the cwm, admiring the forested hills rising up all around, the highest of which is Mynydd Ceiswyn. After 500m, at a fork, go right, following a yellow footpath arrow. On the right-hand side look out for some old slate buildings from the abandoned Ratgoed Quarry, which now have trees growing inside them.

At the next fork, with a ruin ahead, take the left-hand option to pass the ruin and continue ahead, passing **Ratgoed Hall** and following the track towards **Dolgoed**. Just before the track drops down to reach the farmhouse, turn left at a yellow arrow post and follow the edge of the field, with the fence on the right. Ratgoed Hall is the former quarry owner's house. The quarry itself (actually Ralltgoed) was on the Corris tramway, and finally closed in 1946.

After 100m, go through a small black gate on the right with a yellow arrow and follow the path left down a bank to join a track and cross the footbridge over the **Nant Ceiswyn**. Beyond the bridge follow the path left to follow a fence over a stone slab bridge to reach a track; there is a house on the right.

Turn left on the track and follow it ahead, into a forest on the slopes of Mynydd Ffynnonbadarn. 200m after entering the forest, at a fork, go ahead, downhill. After over 1km, the track leaves the forest and farm buildings become visible ahead on the left.

Continue ahead for 100m and take the first track on the right, uphill, shortly before a T-junction. The track zig-zags up, then traverses the slope, passing an old mine entrance and becoming a path.

The path bends left; at a fork, go right, and the path soon heads downhill towards Aberllefenni. Turn right on reaching the road and follow it into the village, passing the old quarry hospital and an information board about the slate industry in the village. Follow this road through the village for approximately 1km and turn left onto a track at the entrance to Foel Friog, where there is a parking sign.

When the track bends left, go ahead down a path where there is an information board. At a track junction, turn left to cross a bridge over the Afon Dulas, then immediately right. Follow this track to the house, head to the right side of the green building, where the streamside path can be picked up to return to Corris.

Walk 29
Aberdyfi

The old shipbuilding town of Aberdyfi sits in a stunning spot, as the Dyfi Estuary meets the sea, bordered by miles of sand dunes and rolling hills. This walk leads up and over a small hill directly above the town and then drops down into the relatively hidden Cwm Maethlon. Following the Afon Dyffryn-gwyn the trail then leaves the valley to reach the sea, spending the last few miles following the beach and the dunes back to the town.

Beginning the descent towards Cwm Maethlon

Start/finish	Tourist Information Centre in Aberdyfi /// outs.extra.grace
Distance	13km (8 miles)
Ascent	300m
Time	4hr
Terrain	Farmland paths, tracks and sandy beach
Maps	OS Explorer Map OL23 Cadair Idris & Llyn Tegid
Access	Aberdyfi is on the coast, west of Machynlleth. There is a car park on the main road, at LL35 0EA.
Facilities	Aberdyfi has shops, pubs and cafés.

From the tourist information centre in **Aberdyfi**, head to the road and turn right; follow the road, with the sea on the right. After 200m, turn left onto the footpath up ramp, doubling back on yourself.

Zig-zag up this path to a road, cross it and continue up. There are steps, which soon become a path. Follow the Welsh Coast Path signs as the path leads clearly up and begins traversing the hillside. The sea is seen on the right, and then the path bends left and a wooded gorge is seen below at **Allt Goch**. The Afon Dyfi Estuary forms part of the border between the counties of Gwynedd, where you are, and Ceredigion, to the south.

Cross the stile next to a wooded stream when it appears,

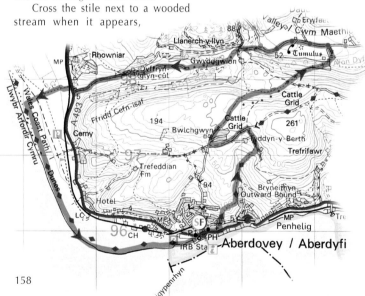

158

cross the footbridge, and head uphill across fields. The path is not clear, but aim for the left-hand side of the farm barns ahead at Erw-pistyll. Head through the gate which appears, to reach a track.

Turn left onto the track and follow it up to the road, past the entrance to **Tyddyn-y-Berth**. Turn left on the road, leaving the Welsh Coast Path. After 500m, at the junction, turn right up towards the chalets. At the fork at the entrance to the site, take the left-hand option through the gate, passing **Bwlchgwyn**. Go ahead along this track and follow it into a field and up to the crest of the hill.

On reaching two gates, go through the left-hand gate/stile and continue straight ahead with the fence on the right. Go through the gate at the end of the field and admire the view ahead over **Cwm Maethlon** and the hills behind. The road through Cwm Maethlon used to be the main route from Machynlleth to Tywyn before the coast road was built via Aberdyfi.

Go straight ahead, down the slope. There is no obvious path. On reaching a fence corner where the slope becomes steeper, turn right and make your way diagonally down a vague grassy ramp towards a gate and ford at the far corner of the field.

At the ford, do not cross it but head through the gate and continue on the path ahead, keeping on the right-hand side of the stream with the fence on the left. The path is grassy and continues on to become a track, which heads downhill past the woodland at Gamallt.

The old track leading down the hillside into Cwm Maethlon

At the **Afon Dyffryn-gwyn**, cross the footbridge and continue ahead past the farm to the road. On the road turn left and follow it for around 1km through Cwm Maethlon, past the **phone box** and the old chapel. The chapel was built in 1810, and also had a school attached, which then educated 30 children. The chapel is now a holiday home.

At the next road junction at Pont Rhyd-y-meirch, turn left, uphill towards **Gwyddgwion** (marked as a track on the map). After 200m the road bends left at a track junction; go straight ahead through a gate onto a track. The track soon disappears but follow the fence on the left through this field. On reaching the gate at the bottom corner, go through it and follow the path onwards between two fences.

This few hundred metres is unmaintained, which is putting it politely. Be ready for vegetation and possibly a stream on the path. If it's too miserable try walking through the field on the right. The path continues between two fences and eventually becomes a reasonable track that arrives at a pond and then the farm at **Dyffryn-glyn-cûl**. Join the tarmac track and follow it through the farm, as it becomes a road. Follow it down to the **A493**.

Turn right onto the road, and then left onto a footpath after 50m. Cross the railway and continue ahead. The path runs in a line to the left of the woodland to reach the golf course. Go through the gate onto the golf course and continue ahead, soon picking up a track that leads ahead towards the sand dunes. Cross the dunes to reach the beach and the sea! In 2012 Wales became the first country in the world to have a publicly accessible path along its whole coast. It runs for 1400km (870 miles).

Turn left on the beach and walk along it, on the **Wales Coast Path** all the way back to Aberdyfi, around 3.5km. If the tide is in you can also walk along the track on the golf course. This leads to a path that runs along next to the railway line. On reaching the caravan site, a path can be followed round to the right of it, following the dunes back to Aberdyfi. Either way, the trail returns to the town beside a large car park and a lifeboat station; turn right here to return to the tourist information centre.

Following the sand dunes along the coast back to Aberdyfi

Machynlleth

The transition between the steeper mountains of Snowdonia and the rolling hills of mid Wales is reasonably clear as you head south of the Afon Dyfi. This walk explores trails through these hills from the ancient town of Machynlleth. With views over the Tarrens and the mighty Dyfi Estuary, it leads through woodland up to Llyn Glanmerin, and then on a straightforward track walk in a loop back down to finish alongside the Dyfi itself, right on the border of the National Park.

Llyn Glanmerin, covered in water lilies, sits in the hills south of Machynlleth

Start/finish	Clock tower at the main road junction in Machynlleth /// gums. jetliner.triads
Distance	14.5km (9 miles)
Ascent	300m
Time	4hr 15min
Terrain	Mostly tracks, with some grassy paths
Maps	OS Explorer Map OL23 Cadair Idris & Llyn Tegid
Access	There is a large pay-and-display car park in the centre of Machynlleth, postcode SY20 8DT.
Facilities	Machynlleth has plenty of shops, pubs and cafes

From the clock tower in **Machynlleth** town centre, head south down Heol Pentrerhedyn past the White Lion Hotel. The road bends right; follow it over three mini roundabouts and past a **school**.

Opposite the sports fields, before the road reaches the main roundabout, turn left at the footpath sign to join a path. This path climbs up steps cut into the rock and passes a bench with a great view back to Machynlleth.

There has been a settlement on the site of **Machynlleth** for thousands of years, but its greatest fame came in 1404 when Owain Glyndŵr was crowned Prince of Wales during his rebellion against English rule. He also held a parliament here, and the building can still be visited in the centre of town. For this reason it is sometimes referred to as the ancient capital of Wales. Being close to the last bridge on the Dyfi before the sea, it has obvious strategic importance, and was even the site of a skirmish during the English Civil War.

On reaching a track by houses at Cae-Gybi Cottages, cross straight over the track and continue on the path. After 150m, join the road and continue ahead uphill. Follow this road for around 1km, past Gelli-lydan, ignoring the route for Glyndwr's Way heading off to the right.

On reaching a road T-junction, turn left and follow the tarmac track with the stream on the right, through Coed Cae-ty up to **Glanmerin Farm**. Once in the farmyard, turn left onto a track, where there is a sign to the lake. Follow the steep track up to a gate and continue ahead on a dirt track. Llyn Glanmerin is also known as Lord Herbert's Lake, who was the owner of Plas Machynlleth at the start of the 20th century.

Head up past a forestry plantation, and at the fork after, take the right-hand option up to a gate. Go through it and continue straight ahead. Follow the vague grassy path to reach a fence/gate. Don't go through the gate, but turn left, to shortly join a line of dirt paths. At the next junction, turn right. The view on the left reaches down over the Dyfi Valley and up to the Tarrens, the most southerly 2000ft mountains in Snowdonia.

Follow this defined dirt track to a fence with a gate; continue ahead through the gate along the bottom of a meadow to reach **Llyn Glanmerin**. After admiring the lake, and the water lilies, follow the path past it to a gate into a forest. After another gate, reach a path junction and turn right.

Follow the stony path through the forest, and at the fork, continue ahead on the right-hand option, following the acorn sign as this is now part of Glyndwr's Way. After a few hundred metres go through the gate into an open area; the path goes ahead, then bends right, traversing round the hillside near Bryn Coch Mawr. It is vague but there are footpath posts.

Descend steeply to a path junction in front of a fence at Bryn Coch Bach and turn left.

Glyndŵr's Way is a 135-mile long distance trail weaving through mid

163

The low rolling hills east of Ffridd Rhiwlwyfen

Wales from Knighton to Welshpool, in a V-shape via Machynlleth. It visits places associated with Owain Glyndŵr.

After around 300m, on reaching a substantial track, turn left uphill, then after less than 50m, turn right onto a level path. Follow this path, which runs along a fence, bends left and reaches a set of gates. Go ahead through the small gate and continue on to reach the farmhouse at **Rhiwlwyfen**. Follow the track past it, which becomes tarmac.

Follow the tarmac track downhill for over 1km downhill; when it flattens out, you'll reach two gates near Coed Pandy-bâch, where the right-hand gate leads onto the road. Go through the left-hand gate, where there is a footpath sign, onto a grassy path. Follow this path ahead and then down, roughly following the fence.

The path swings in a loop downhill and comes to a fence corner. Continue ahead, and when the vegetation allows turn right, downhill, to the right of the **golf course** to reach the road near where the cattle grid is marked on the 1:25,000 OS map.

Turn right on the road, and when the road bends right after 100m, turn left onto a tarmac track that goes down in between houses at Dol-gau. As this track bends right to enter a garden, turn left through a gate, following a footpath arrow, then almost immediately turn right to pass to the left of a barn. On reaching the track by the **Afon Dulas**, turn left.

The path runs alongside the Afon Dyfi towards Machynlleth

Follow the river through fields and across the main road, then continue on the path next to the river all the way to a caravan park, which is around 500m after the main road. The area in between the river and the bank can be quite overgrown, so it is easier to walk on the top of the bank, but on reaching the caravan park fence, it is necessary to descend the bank to the right and find the gate, near the river. Go through it and follow the path ahead.

At the track, follow it up to the tarmac and turn right (ahead); the track rises up, and at the fork, go right. Descend and take the next track on the right, down to the river. Turn left onto a path, and after crossing a stile, enter a field with a house ahead on the right. Go straight ahead, following the track that runs on the right-hand side of a woodland around **Garth**.

Go through the gate at the top left of the field and then through another gate 20m away across a track. Join a path leading right, through woods. The path leads down to cross the railway and reaches the **Afon Dyfi** ('dark river'). The Dyfi Estuary is a designated UNESCO biosphere reserve because of its near-pristine wildlife habitat in the form of salt marsh, sandy estuary and oak woodlands.

Follow the riverside path, passing a footbridge. Stay on the left side of the river until reaching the A487 road leading over the bridge Pont ar Ddyfi. Turn left and follow the road back to the clock tower in Machynlleth.

Appendix A
Useful contacts

Tourist information
Snowdonia National Park Visitor Centre,
Aberdyfi
Wharf Gardens
Sea View Terrace
Aberdyfi
LL35 0ED
tel 01654 767321

Coed y Brenin Forest Park Visitor Centre
tel 01341 440747
www.visitsnowdonia.info/
coed-y-brenin-forest-park

Owain Glyndŵr's Parliament House
93 Heol Maengwyn
Machynlleth
SY20 8EE
www.canolfanglyndwr.org

Harlech Castle (has a good information
centre)
Harlech
LL46 2YH
tel 01766 780552
www.cadw.gov.wales/visit/
places-to-visit/harlech-castle

Bala Lake Railway
tel 01678 540666
www.bala-lake-railway.co.uk

Talyllyn Railway
tel 01654 710472
www.talyllyn.co.uk

Cycling
Dolgellau Cycles (if you want to hire
bikes to cycle the Mawddach Trail)
The Old Furnace
Smithfield St

Dolgellau
LL40 1DE
tel 01341 423332
www.dolgellaucycles.co.uk

You can find more information on local
cycling routes and hire locations at
http://mawddachestuary.co.uk/cycling/
index.html

Weather forecasts
Mountain Weather Information Service
www.mwis.org.uk

Met Office Mountain Weather
www.metoffice.gov.uk/public/weather/
mountain-forecasts

BBC Weather
www.bbc.co.uk/weather

Transport
Traveline Cymru
tel 0800 464 0000
www.traveline.cymru

Accommodation
Visit Snowdonia
www.visitsnowdonia.info

Youth Hostels Association
www.yha.org.uk

Independent Hostels UK
www.independenthostels.co.uk

NOTES

Explore the world with Cicerone

walking • trekking • mountaineering • climbing • mountain biking •
cycling • via ferratas • scrambling • trail running • skills and techniques

For over 50 years, Cicerone have built up an outstanding collection of
nearly 400 guides, inspiring all sorts of amazing experiences.

www.cicerone.co.uk – where adventures begin

- Our **website** is a treasure-trove for every outdoor adventurer. You
  can buy books or read inspiring articles and trip reports, get technical
  advice, check for updates, and view videos, photographs and mapping
  for routes and treks.

- **Register this book** or any other Cicerone guide in your member's
  library on our website and you can choose to automatically access
  updates and GPX files for your books, if available.

- Our **fortnightly newsletters** will update you on new publications and
  articles and keep you informed of other news and events. You can also
  follow us on Facebook, Twitter and Instagram.

We hope you have enjoyed using this guidebook. If you have any
comments you would like to share, please contact us using the form on
our website or via email, so that we can provide the best experience for
future customers.

CICERONE

Juniper House, Murley Moss Business Village, Oxenholme Road, Kendal LA9 7RL

✉ info@cicerone.co.uk   cicerone.co.uk